Passing the Guard

Ed Beneville
and
Tim Cartmell

WARNING:

Practice of the material in this book is inherently dangerous and could cause injury or death. Martial arts should be practiced under the guidance of a qualified instructor. Be mindful to avoid injuring yourself or others practicing the material in this book. The authors and Grappling Arts Publications, LLC, deny any liability for the use or misuse of the material herein. Consult a physician before engaging in the activities demonstrated in this book. Train smart.

CREDITS

This book was conceived, written and produced by Ed Beneville and Tim Cartmell. The lion's share of the photography is by Shane Lindsay. Additional photographs were taken by Amber Cartmell and Maynard Ancheta.

The book was produced over the course of many moons in the spare time of the authors, and sometimes at the expense of their other jobs. The pictures were photographed at Tim Cartmell's Shen Wu Academy of Martial Arts in Garden Grove, California. The book was produced on PCs with digital cameras and Adobe software.

ABOUT THIS BOOK

This book was written with the assumption that intensivity typically prevails over extensivity. Rather than trying to touch upon all that is Brazilian Jiu-Jitsu, we have focused on one area - passing the guard - and tried to cover it well. This book also attempts to address various situations, opportunities, and dangers, which occur in the process of passing guard.

It is hoped that this book will serve as a valuable resource to jiu-jitsu, judo, and sambo players, as well as grapplers and martial artists in general. The rules and strategies discussed throughout the book were written with Brazilian Jiu-Jitsu sport competition in mind. Their application, however, is much broader.

The level of material ranges from rudimentary to advanced. We make little attempt to differentiate on the basis of difficulty. What is hard for one comes easily to another. We have tried to cover the fundamentals, but that is no easy task. To a large extent, martial arts can only be learned by doing. This applies to fundamental and advanced technique alike. This book is not a substitute for training, or for the feedback of someone who knows what they are talking about. No book or video is. On the other hand, this is a source of information, some of which is not widely taught or easily available..

It is our experience that if you are taught the same technique by three different instructors, each is likely to teach details that the others did not. To the extent that this book covers techniques that you are already acquainted with, we hope this will be the case for you.

It would have been cumbersome to both the reader and the authors to cover everything that is important every time it is important. It is the nature of grappling that the principles and details which make one technique work, have applications to other techniques. Learning to improvise the details and principles learned from one technique into other situations is vital to proficiency in the art, not to mention a big part of what makes it interesting. Grappling arts require both mental and physical acumen. This book provides ideas which have applications beyond what is shown. Experiment with them, modify them, and make them your own.

All of the techniques in this book work. But none of them work if improperly executed. The difference between success and failure of a technique sometimes comes down to a single detail. Do not give up on a technique because it is not immediately successful. It may be that you have forgot something, your timing is off, or your opponent is a step ahead of you.

Different physical attributes favor different techniques. Every player must make adjustments for their own attributes, as well as those of their opponent. Keep this in mind as you attempt to apply techniques.

We have tried to make the demonstration of technique primarily visual. To that end the book is picture intensive. Text is provided and the text is important. Nevertheless, many readers will focus most of their attention almost exclusively on the pictures. Realizing this, and to facilitate visual learning, we did several things. Typically, martial arts books (and "how to" books generally) rely on numbered pictures with corresponding numbered text. The result is that it takes some effort for the reader to figure out the sequence of the pictures and the corresponding text. We have attempted to alleviate this difficulty with a non-numeric system. The order of the pictures for a technique is delineated by lines and symbols to make recognizing their flow intuitive and obvious. Many of the techniques are shown from more than one angle. Where more than one angle is shown, the alternate views are delineated by symbols. Finally, we have highlighted key points and the direction of certain movements by illustrating some of the photos.

The names given to the techniques in this book are a mixture of convention and imagination. English, Portuguese, and Japanese terms are used. If you are unfamiliar with some of our terminology, it may be because we made it up.

We hope that this book proves to be a valuable resource and that it expands your game. We plan on authoring future books on the other aspects of Brazilian Jiu Jitsu.

ACKNOWLEDGEMENTS

ED

I have studied jiu-jitsu under Joe Moreira (sixth degree black belt) for the past five plus years. A great deal of what is contained in this book is knowledge passed to me by him. Joe's depth of martial arts know how continues to amaze me. Some say that by the time you reach purple belt you have already seen most of what there is to know and that higher rank is mostly a matter of experience and refinement. My experience has been that there is always more to know, a fact which Joe has demonstrated through his instruction time and time again.

My interest in jiu-jitsu began when I watched Royce Gracie compete in the Ultimate Fighting Championships. I was awed at his ability to use technique to defeat fighters who appeared physically superior. Watching him, the efficacy of the art was immediately apparent. I haven not studied directly under members of the Gracie family, but tip my hat to them. Their enormous contributions to the art cannot be denied; without the Gracies, there would be no Brazilian Jiu-Jitsu.

My first exposure to the sportive aspect of Brazilian Jiu-Jitsu was as a spectator at one of Joe Moreira's international tournaments. I went there with my friend Anthony Peters. I did not imagine at the time that I would some day be one of the competitors, much less that I would I would enjoy success as a competitor. Thanks Tony.

My first experience in a jiu-jitsu class was with Cleber Luciano at the now defunct Brazilian Martial Arts Academy of Huntington Beach. I picked up a flyer at a bagel shop and saw that the location was convenient. I was hooked after the first class. Though Cleber was just learning English at the time, he instilled part of his own love for the art to me. For that, I am indebted to him.

Over the years I have been fortunate to learn from many good teachers. I've found that just about everyone who has practiced for years has something valuable they can teach you. All of the following are instructors who have taught me. All contributed to some degree to what I know about jiu-jitsu and the content of this book. They are, in no particular order: Gustavo (Moreira) Froes, James Boran, Kenny Kallenberger, Paulo Gazze Jr., Juliano Prado, Carlos Augusto, Aloisio Silva, Marcos Vinicius, Nori Bunasawa, Brad Jackson, Dave Dartangion, and Randy Bloom.

Finally, a nod to my training partners many of whom have forced me to raise my game by kicking my ass.

No doubt there will be those who question who I am to make a book such as this. I make no claim to knowing more than any of those who have taught me martial arts, to the contrary. I produced this book because I believe that you should follow your bliss, and I love jiu-jitsu. I produced this book because I wanted to try something completely different (this time desktop publishing) as is my practice every five years or so. I produced this book because I did not believe that anyone else was about to. Since this project began, other books on Brazilian Jiu-Jitsu have hit the market. Still, they are different sorts of books than this one.

TIM

I have been practicing Brazilian Jiu Jitsu since 1995. I have had the good fortune to study under some fine teachers, both Brazilian and American. I would like to thank everyone who has taught and trained with me and give special thanks to a few individuals who have been the most instrumental in my training. First off, I'd like to thank my friend and first training partner, Glen Rosenzweig. Glen and I began to practice BJJ together, and have trained together ever since.

I would like to thank Joe Moreira and his students for the years I spent training in Joe's school. Finally, my heartfelt appreciation and thanks to Cleber Luciano, who has been my teacher for the last several years. Cleber has had the greatest influence on my Jiu Jitsu practice, and has without fail proven to be a most excellent instructor.

The authors would like to express their appreciation to **Shane Lindsay** for his dedicated efforts as the photographer. Thanks Shane!

❖ CONTENTS ❖

1. FUNDAMENTALS   1

2. PASSING FROM THE KNEES   16

3. STANDING PASSES   57

4. DEFENSES AND COUNTERS   93

5. THE HALF GUARD   131

6. ATTACKS   146

7. THE TURTLE POSITION   159

8. DRILLS   191

❖ LEGEND ❖

primary view

 path starts

 path ends

 path turns - *down and to left*

 path resumes - *from up and to right*

path goes two ways

━━━ path - connects the sequence of pictures

alternative view

 path starts

 path ends

 path turns - *down and to left*

 path rusumes - *from up and to right*

━━━ alternative view - connected frames show the same action from a different view

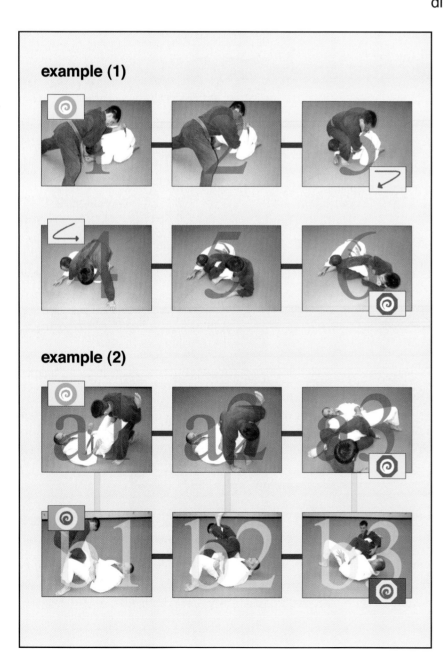

example (1)

example (2)

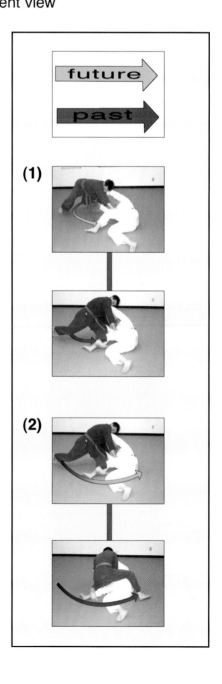

CHAPTER 1

ON PASSING THE GUARD...

Anyone who has been exposed to Brazilian Jiu Jitsu immediately becomes aware of the importance of the Guard position. Fighting in the Guard position will occur in almost all Jiu Jitsu matches. Very often the match will be decided by one's ability to pass the Guard. Since there are more attacks from the Guard position than any other position on the ground, it becomes vital that the fighter in the Guard becomes proficient at passing. When fighting a skilled fighter, especially one who has a good Guard, passing the Guard can become very difficult. It is important to have at least several methods of passing, and to be able to flow from one technique to the other as smoothly as possible.

A number of variables must be consided when passing the Guard. When inside an opponent's Closed Guard, there are very few options for attack. So, the first skill is to be able to break an opponent's feet open. Once the opponent's feet are open, the opportunity to either pass the Guard or attack the legs is created. At all times, you must be on guard against the opponent's attack as you attempt to pass. In addition, you need to be able to pass the Guard when caught in submission positions. You must be ready for sweeps and reversals that put you on your back with the opponent on top, or your opponent on your back. As you come close to passing, you need to maintain control and keep the opponent from escaping or back rolling to the knees to avoid being passed. You also have the option of attacking the opponent's legs with a variety of submission techniques: foot locks, toe holds or knee bars etc.

There are two factors that are primary for success in passing the Guard. The first is balance, or base. At all times, you must maintain a strong and balanced position. This usually requires constant adjustment on your part, depending both on what you are trying to do and what the opponent is doing. This brings up the second primary factor, sensitivity. Your opponent will be doing everything he can to stop you from passing the Guard, while at the same time setting up his own offensive techniques. It is extremely important to pay constant attention to the opponent's position, movement, grips and the amount and direction of pressure applied. When you can constantly adjust to your opponent's movement and technique, and use it to set up your own techniques, you will be able to pass the Guard smoothly and quickly.

There are several basic strategies for passing the Guard. Variables such as size, strength, flexibility and endurance can be brought into play depending on the type of opponent you are fighting. By being proficient at a number of different strategies and techniques, you can use your relative strengths to your advantage. For example, if you are larger and heavier than your opponent, you can use your weight to smash the opponent and pass. If you are smaller and lighter than your opponent, you can use your speed to pass. It is important to master several different strategies and techniques so that you are prepared for the variety of opponent's you are likely to face. Even within the same weight class, you will most likely meet opponents that are considerably stronger or weaker than you, who are more or less flexible than you, etc. You need to be flexible in your game to adjust to different kinds of fighters. Finally, in competitive matches, the score and time remaining will also influence your strategy and the types of technique used.

Conclusion: Whether or not you ever become proficient at a wide variety of passes, you should be aware of many strategies and techniques. By doing so you will be better equiped to attack and defend the vast myriad of variables and situations which you will sooner or later face.

POSTURE AND BASE

Above all else, your posture and base (balance) will determine your success in passing the Guard. Without balance, your opponent will have little trouble applying a submission or a sweep. Without base, you will not have the power to open your opponent's feet and control him as you pass. The correct alignment of your torso and limbs and the ability to constantly adjust your position to maintain balance are key to a successful passing. In order to maintain balance and a strong position, you will need to be relaxed. Relaxation will allow you to move freely and quickly, while simultaneously remaining sensitive to your opponent's movements and attacks.

The most important factor determining whether or not your structure is strong and balanced is the placement of your head. Since your head is at the top of your spine, the placement and movement of the head directly influence the entire balance of the body. In general, you want to stretch your spine to its full length, and lift up from the crown of your head, keeping your chin slightly tucked in when beginning a pass from the guard. Once you collapse your chest and slump over forward, you will lose the ability to generate force, and it will be easier for the opponent to control and move you. When in the Guard, a slumped over posture makes it especially easy for your opponent to pull your head down for a choke or to set up an armbar or triangle choke.

When sitting in the opponent's Guard, before you start your pass, you should begin sitting on your heels with a fairly wide base, knees spread apart. The wider the base, the greater the stability. Your head should be up with the back straight, your hands on the opponent in an appropriate grip position. Your body should resemble the shape of a pyramid, with the head positioned at about the mid-point between your hands and feet.

Grips need to be taken carefully in order to guard against loss of balance and to prevent submissions. Extending the arm too far up the opponent's body in the wrong positions, or holding with the elbows opened out to the sides, can leave you vulnerable to wrist, elbow, and shoulder, submissions. In general, the elbows should be closed inward and kept down and 'heavy.' The wrists should not be bent too far upward or downward. The hands grip the opponent's body

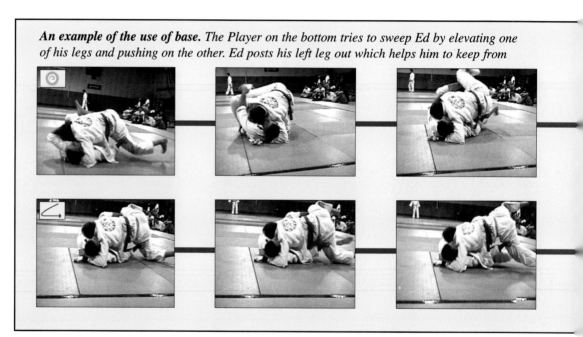

An example of the use of base. The Player on the bottom tries to sweep Ed by elevating one of his legs and pushing on the other. Ed posts his left leg out which helps him to keep from

and limbs, and are rarely placed on the mat. Remember, the position of the grip will determine not only the options available to pass, but also your overall stability. The position of your arms should always act to strengthen your base, your arm often acting as a "third leg." This becomes especially important when changing the position of your base or when stepping with the feet.

Let's discuss the center of gravity (COG). We all know that the lower the center of gravity and the wider the base, the more stable the object. Obviously, since our goal is not to sit motionless in the Guard but to pass it or counter-attack, we need to find the dynamic balance between stability and mobility. Generally, we need to keep our COG as low as possible, even as we move. This is usually accomplished by keeping the hips lower than the head. There are, of course, exceptions. These less commonly seen techniques involve "jumping" over the guard with the hips rising high. These techniques are inherently unstable and must be used with the correct timing and position.

Besides keeping the weight low, many Guard pass techniques will involve forward pressure and "smashing" the opponent with your weight. Since

posture and stable COG, you will be able to use the power of your legs to press your weight into the opponent for control, or to help you maneuver quickly around the opponent.

Maintaining your balance while in movement is vital. As you pass the guard, you can use your feet, knees, hips, shoulders, elbows or head, to post on the ground or your opponent to make a base. Standing up without an appropriate grip leaves you vulnerable to sweeps. You should typically have at least one hand gripping or posting on the opponent at all times as you pass the guard. Think of a table, it is most stable with its four legs in place. If one leg is broken off, the table will still be relatively stable. A table balanced on two legs is extremely unstable and a small amount of force will cause it to tip over and fall. Not only your hands and feet but also your knees, hips, shoulders, elbows and head can be used to post on the opponent or the mat. Try to have at least three if not four points stabilizing your base as you position and pass the Guard.

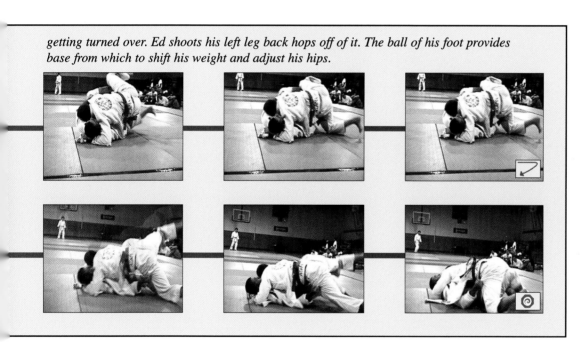

getting turned over. Ed shoots his left leg back hops off of it. The ball of his foot provides base from which to shift his weight and adjust his hips.

One final point. When you are attempting to pass the Guard, and the opponent begins to compromise your base, or you feel as if your balance is threatened, consider coming back to a stable base position to prevent a sweep or submission, before resuming the Guard pass.

you are either on your knees or standing when you pass, you have the advantage of gravity on your side. By remaining relaxed, with the COG low and pressing into the opponent, you can conserve energy while forcing your opponent to work hard in order to maintain his position. In addition, your upright position when passing allows you to use not only the weight of your center against the opponent, but also the power of your legs. It will be difficult to control an opponent's hips and legs with the strength of your arms alone. But with correct

When sitting in your opponent's guard, keep your back straight, your rear sitting over your feet and your arms in an appropriate grip on the opponent's body. Although the hand and leg placement will vary according to the situation and technique applied, some fundamental alignments should be maintained. First, the overall alignment of the body is 'pyramid' shaped. Viewed from the side, the head should be near the midpoint between the hands and the feet. Leaning too far forward or backward compromises the base and makes it difficult to either control the opponent's movement or defend against his attacks. Here, we see Blue sitting in with good posture. Wwith a grip under White's armpits, Blue is holdling the gi and keeping his elbows in tight to White's body, making it difficult for White to attack his arm, sit up to attack the neck, or sweep. At this point, Blue keeps his knees outside of White's hips and his back straight.

@ Keep your hands in front of your head.

@ Keep your knees wide apart.

@ Your butt is low and your back is straight.

@ Putting your hands in his armpits is relatively safe position for your arms while you adjust the rest of your base and prepare for your next move.

▲ Blue holds under White's armpits with the four fingers inside the armpits and the thumb hooked over the top of White's shoulders.

▼ Alternatively, he makes his hands into fists.

EXAMPLES OF BAD POSTURE AND HAND PLACEMENT.

◄ Here, White has his center too high, and his head too far forward (directly over his hands). He is susceptible to being off balanced to his front. With his butt so high, being swept is a concern.

◄ With his head so far forward and his center of gravity high, Blue can easily reach up and grab White's lapel. White has his head up, which is good. It is the position of the hand relative to his head which will give White problems.

┌─────────────────────────────┐
│ ◉ Keep your hands in front │
│ of your head. White has │
│ poor base with his head │
│ past the vertical plane │
│ running from his hands. │
└─────────────────────────────┘

◄ Blue pulls White down into a choke...

◄ or controls his head.

▲ Here White holds the belt with his wrists bent, which is a weak grip.

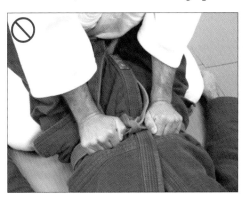

▲ This is a front view of the incorrect, bent wrist grip.

▲ With White's wrists bent too far, it is easy for Blue to pull White forward. Pulling White's elbow from over the top is an easy way to break White down.

◉ Blue puts on a wristlock by jamming White's elbow into his stomach to put pressure on the wrist.

HOW TIGHTLY TO GRIP.

If you grip the opponent's gi too tightly, it is easy to fatigue your hands. Sensitivity to when a tight grip is desirable saves energy. If your opponent is not fighting your grip don't tire your fingers by over gripping. That being said, you must stay ready to tighten your grip if the opponent tries to force his way free of your grip and you do not want him to. Most players give clues before they try to break free; learn to spot them.

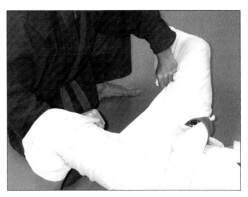

This is the proper way to grip the legs when passing the guard. The thumbs are turned back toward yourself with the palms down, and the wrists are kept straight.

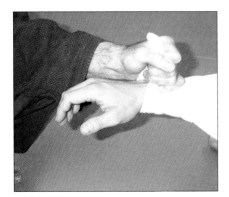

This method involves gripping the cloth with the four fingers wrapped inside the material, thumb on the outside.

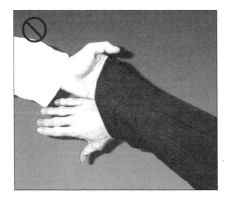

This is an illegal grip. It is against the rules to grab inside the sleeves.

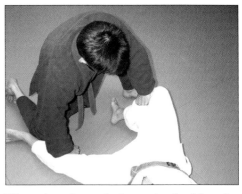

Note that the grip is to the inside of the knees. This affords control. From this inside grip it is easy for Blue to switch his grip or wrap his hands under White's legs.

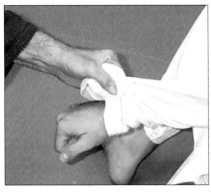

With this grip, the hand holds around the cloth with all fingers outside of the material.

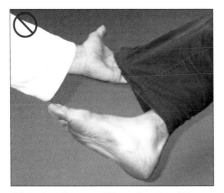

This is also an illegal grip. You cannot grab inside the cuff. One reason these grips are forbidden is because of the potential danger to the fingers if the opponent twists his arm or leg. That being said, they are effective if the opponent does not twist his limb, and sometimes even if they do.

This is an incorrect way to hold the legs when passing the guard. It is awkward and puts to much pressure on the wrist.

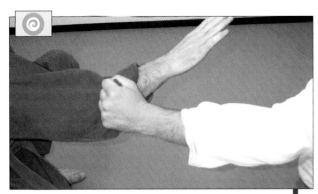

White grabs the outside of Blue's sleeve.

Blue circles his hand over the top to the outside of White's wrist, turning his thumb down.

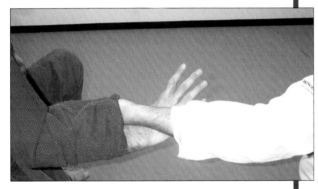

Blue continues to circle his hand up inside White's wrist.

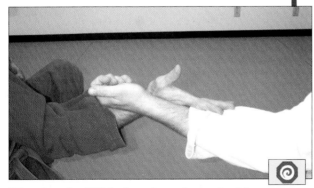

Blue breaks White's grip as he twist his hand palm up over the top of White's wrist.

WHAT IS THE GUARD?

There are two main types of Guard:

Closed Guard is when a fighter wraps his legs around his opponent's torso and locks his feet behind the opponent's back. The fighter in the Guard can either be on his knees or standing.

Open Guard is when a fighter lays on his back with his feet open, preventing the opponent from passing around his legs.

Spider Guard is a variety of Open Guard. Other variations include, the Butterfly Guard (pg. 129), and De La Riva style (pg. 127).

STAGGERING HANDS

In order to keep yourself from getting pulled down, stagger your hands. This provides for good base while at the same time allowing you to work one arm back to help with opening up the legs.

Here we see a correct way to grip in the guard. Blue has his hands staggered, the left hand holding the lapel at the lower chest and his right hand holing at the hip. This grip allows Blue to control White's movement, limit White's ability to attack while maintaining his own base in preparation for breaking the guard. Notice how Blue keeps his elbows locked in tightly. Note also that he is gripping the gi pants.

Keep your knees wide and your butt down.

❷ It is helpful to be able to use your insteps for base. If you cannot, work on it. Eventually (after plenty of cramps in your arches) the flexibility will come... eventually.

There are a number of good grips for the forward hand. Here both of White's lapels are taken.

❷ Grabbing either lapel or the cloth works also. If Blue did not hold on at all White could easily pull Blue's arm into a position to attack it.

❷ Notice how Blue keeps his right elbow in tight and pressing down inside White's left thigh. This prevents White from pulling Blue's arm in for an armbar or triangle choke, while helping to limit White's mobility. Notice also that Blue keeps forward pressure with his left hand, preventing White from moving forward to attack.

◀▶ Blue pushes White away with his hands as he brings his left knee into the center of White's rear.

◀▶ With his leg wedged in place and White's hip movement controlled by the downward pressure of his arms, Blue opens his right leg back to make space to for hips to move.

◀▶ Blue sits back and twists his hips to the right, continuing to push forward and downward with his left hand as his right elbow presses downward into White's knee, opening the guard.

🌀 Here White fails to do anything to put downward pressure on Blue's hips. Blue easily counters the attempt to break open his legs by lifting his butt ontop of White's thigh.

Here Blue breaks open the guard by jamming the points of his elbows into White's quadriceps. Blue sinks the weight of his upper body into his elbows.

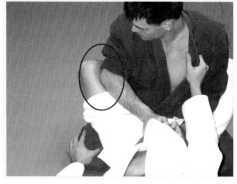

Note how Blue's elbow presses into the sensitive area at the inside of White's lower thigh.

Usually the bottom player will open his guard rather than withstand the pain.

❷ Note that the hands are not staggered during this technique. There are few absolutes in Jiu Jitsu. Sometimes it is useful to pass this way. Blue is more susceptible to being pulled forward, however.

▶ Blue pushes White away with his hands as he brings his left knee into the center of White's rear.

▶ With his leg wedged in place and White's hip movement controlled by the downward pressure of Blue's arms, Blue opens his right leg back to make space to for hips to move.

▶ Blue sits back and twists his hips to the right, continuing to push forward and downward with his left hands as his right elbow presses downward into White's left knee...

▶ ... opening the guard.

❷ This technique combines the one to the left with that of the preceding page.

Blue sets his base and controls White by gripping under his armpits. Be sure to keep your elbows in.

Blue begins to shoot his hips backward while pushing forward under White's armpits, putting pressure against White's calves.

Continuing the backward thrust of the hips and forward push of the arms, Blue breaks the guard.

Blue sits in base and holds under White's armpits.

Blue stands and wedges his left knee directly in the center of White' rear. Ideally Blue's patella pushes right into White's tailbone.

Blue sits back over his left leg, bringing his torso up straight and causing White to slide down the outside of his left shin, the pressure breaking the guard. *This pass is especially useful when the opponent locks his legs high around your ribs.*

THE CAN OPENER

Blue grabs the back of White's head with both hands and the heels of his palms at the base of White's head. Blue pinches his elbows in close together and squeezes his wrists together against the sides of White's neck (it is very important not to leave space between your wrists and the opponent's neck). Blue keeps his elbows close together and pressed against the front of White's chest.

Blue pulls back with both hands, forcing White's chin against his chest as he simultaneously drives his elbows into White's chest. The pressure causes the back of White's neck to be stretched painfully. This technique may cause the opponent to submit, but is most often used as a method of breaking he opponent's Guard (the opponent will be forced to open his Guard and push you away to relieve the pressure on his neck).

◄ Blue controls White's hips with his right hand.

◄ Blue lifts his right leg, placing the sole on the mat at his right side, far enough back so that White cannot grab his ankle. Blue is careful to keep his back straight and weight down.

◄ Raising his hips straight up, Blue places his left hand on the inside of White's right knee.

◄ Blue presses straight downward on White's leg (using a rapid bouncing motion if necessary) to begin sliding White's leg down to the mat.

> ☯ Notice that Blue's left arm is straight and he is using his body weight and not the strength of his left arm alone to pin White's leg down.

◄ White's feet break apart and Blue pins White's right leg to the mat with his left arm.

▲Blue controls White's hips.

▲Blue shifts his left hip back while maintaining pressure on Whites hips. It is important to first move the left hip back with this pass.

▲▼Blue holds White's hips to the mat and now twists his body to the right, simultaneously lifting his right knee outward and upward to break the guard.

More information on freeing and protecting the arms while passing the guard appears in Chapter 5, *Defenses andCounters*.

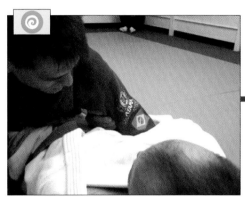  

White wraps Blue's left arm tightly, preparing to attack.

Blue leans to his right, rolls his left shoulder over and lifts his left elbow.

Pulling up sharply with his left elbow, Blue jerks his arm free.

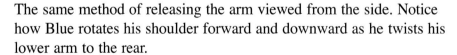

The same method of releasing the arm viewed from the side. Notice how Blue rotates his shoulder forward and downward as he twists his lower arm to the rear.

Here White is making the mistake of reaching his arm in too high, towards Blue's head. Making matters worse he is leaving his right arm behind without doing anything to control Blue's left leg. This is a common novice mistake.

With the arm extended, it is easy for Blue to catch White in a Triangle choke...

... or an armbar.

◁**Close Range:** When the fighters are chest to chest.

This position is disadvantageous for the fighter attempting to pass.

▷**Base in the Guard:** When the fighter in the guard is sitting up straight in base, with the guard closed.

This is a more neutral position, but the fighter on his back has the option to attack.

◁**Medium Range:** When the fighter in the guard has broken the opponent's feet open, but remains close to the opponent's hips.

This is a relatively neutral position, with the fighter on his back in position to attack but now the fighter on his knees is in position to pass or counter-attack.

▷**Long Range:** When the fighter in the guard has backed away from the opponent's hips and has cleared his feet.

This is a somewhat neutral position, with the same options as the medium range. Blue is better off than White. White does not have much control; Blue has space and mobility to pass.

CHAPTER 2

OVERVIEW

There are many ways to pass the Guard and many possible submission opportunities once the opponent's feet are open. There are two basic positions from which the Guard is passed, standing and from the knees. Kneeling passes allow you to keep your center of gravity low, and your base wide. Standing passes allow you to put more downward crushing pressure on the opponent and mobility is greater.

There are three basic methods for passing the Guard: under the legs, over the legs, or around the legs. Techniques can and should be used in combination. Once the opponent's feet are open, opportunities for leg submissions presents themselves. During the pass, there is opportunity to set up foot locks, knee bars, toe holds, key locks and heel hooks.

It is important to be proficient at several different ways to pass the Guard. It is unlikely you will be able to pass the Guard of a skilled opponent with the first pass attempted. Very often, especially with a strong opponent, your best chance of passing is to flow with his technique and take the opponent given. A flexible strategy is usually best, unless you can dominate an opponent with strength or weight. Another strategy that can be employed, especially as a last resort is to bait the opponent with an opportunity for submission, and then pass as he attacks. For example, you extend your arm up high, wait for the opponent to attack with an armbar and then defend the armbar, giving you an opportunity to pass. This is a delicate game; the threat of submission is close. Although less commonly seen, passes that involve jumping over the opponent or rolling over have a surprise element and sometimes provide the best means to pass. It is good to be

familiar with jumping and rolling passes.

When you are larger and stronger than your opponent, passes that are based on crushing or smashing the opponent are often best applied. These types of passes require constant forward pressure and weight. When facing a larger or stronger opponent, passes involving speed may be a better choice.

This chapter will focus on passes from the knees. We begin perhaps the most basic of the passes. It is also one of the most reliable and effective, with or without the gi.

Do not mistake basic moves as being one's that will not work against a skilled opponent. Sometimes basic is best. Of course, if you are limited to one or two passes and your opponent knows it, that can be a problem. Also keep in mind that even simple moves sometimes have many fine points, any one of which can mean the difference between success and failure.

PASSING THE GUARD FROM THE KNEES

The most basic Guard passes are from the knees. Most beginners will learn to break the Guard while on the knees, and then pass the Guard while keeping one knee on the mat. Breaking and passing the Guard from the knees is more stable than standing to pass, the center of gravity is lower and the base much wider. Although you can of course be swept from the knees, because of the lower center of gravity, you will usually be more successful at stopping sweep attempts. On the other hand, the risk of getting caught in an armbar, choke or triangle is somewhat higher when passing low, on the knees. The downside to the increased stability of low Guard passes is the decrease in potential speed. Just as we can obviously run faster on our feet than on our knees, you will not have the same speed and ability for rapid changes in direction you would have standing.

One advantage of passing from the knees is conservation of energy. In general, it requires less energy to pass from the knees than standing. This will become an important factor in matches where you are already fatigued, but need to pass the Guard (when you are down on points for example). In addition, the majority of low passes involve staying very close and tight to the opponent's hips. Controlling the opponent's hips greatly restricts his freedom of motion, while at the same time allowing you to use gravity and your weight to your advantage. You can conserve your own energy while forcing the opponent to constantly work against your weight. If you are stronger and heavier than your opponent, these types of passes may be most effective for you.

Passing close to the opponent on the knees also limits the variations of the Guard available to the opponent. For example, passing close and low prevents the opponent from using the Spider Guard (feet on your biceps) or De La Riva Guards (leg threaded through your legs from the rear). If the opponent has his foot or feet hooked inside your legs, staying low will also make it difficult for him to lift you with elevator type sweeps. It will be very difficult for your opponent to set up leg submissions while you are passing low. It will also be more difficult for you to set up footlocks if you stay low and close to your opponent as you pass.

It may be more difficult to open the opponent's Guard while on the knees. The opponent will be able to keep his hips on the mat for the most part increasing his potential power, and, because of your limited mobility, he will be able to adjust his position as you attempt to open his Guard. Once the opponent's Guard is open, if you stay on your knees he will be better able to re-lock his Guard than if you are standing. This is an important consideration when fighting an opponent that prefers to attack from a closed Guard.

Once the guard is open, Blue begins to reach his right arm under and around White's left leg, making sure he keeps his left elbow down and tight inside White's right leg.

Continuing, Blue presses his chest behind White's left leg, beginning to smash White's leg into his own chest. Blue stays low, making White's left leg slide up onto the top of his shoulder where he will be able to use the power of his legs and body to lift and smash the leg, rather than the power of his arm alone.

Blue lifts his knees off the mat and pushes off with the balls of his feet in order to increase his forward power and bring more weight onto White's leg. Blue grabs inside of White's right lapel with the thumb in.

GETTING THE HEAD AROUND THE LEG

◄Blue has his right arm underhooking White's left leg and has a grip on White's far lapel. Blue has begun to pass the Guard and is smashing White with his weight.

▼Blue continues to move up toward White's head. Blue has turned his head to look away from White's head, which helps Blue drop more of his weight into White's chest as well as clearing his head so that White's leg will slide off his shoulder.

▶White's leg slips past Blue's head and Blue continues to smash his right shoulder into White's chest to complete the Guard pass. Note that there is constant forward pressure on White throughout the technique.

Blue continues to smash White's leg into his chest, attempting to press White's left knee into his face.

Blue pulls himself down and around White's left leg to pass.

Forward pressure from beginning to end!

GETTING THE OPPONENT'S LEG UP ON YOUR SHOULDER.

Here are multiple views of the action of the arm during the smash guard pass.

Notice how Blue lowers his level to slide White's leg on top of his shoulder. It is important not to try to lift the opponent's leg with your arm power or from the crease of your elbow. By sliding the leg up onto your shoulder, you can lift the opponent's leg with the power of your legs and hips.

Blue keeps his left elbow down and pulled back, preventing White from pulling his arm in for a Triangle.

Blue grabs White's cross collar thumb in.

Blue sprawls his weight onto White, smashing him in preparation for the pass and **maintaining constant forward pressure.**

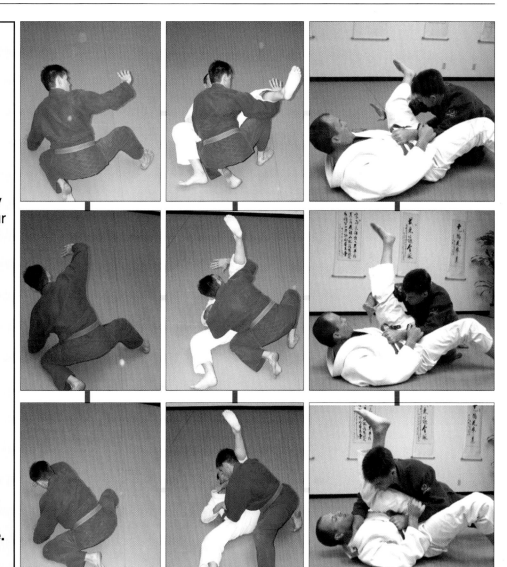

❷ This technique works in combination with the Smash Pass on the preceding page.

▶ As Blue attempts to smash and pass, White stops him by pushing on his hip and shoulder.

▶ Maintaining his grip on White's lapel, and pulling himself forward, Blue slides his left knee over the top of White's thigh, pressing his hips close in to White's hips and pressing his chest forward and downward.

▶ Blue reaches his left arm underneath White's neck and pulls himself downward chest to chest as he steps back over White's leg with his right leg, keeping his left foot hooked over the top of White's right thigh in order to maintain control of White's hips.

▶ Posting on the ball of his right foot, Blue steps his left leg underneath his right and squares his hips.

▶ Blue finishes by bringing his right knee up against White's left hip and into side control. Blue takes his right arm from between White's legs and uses it to help control.

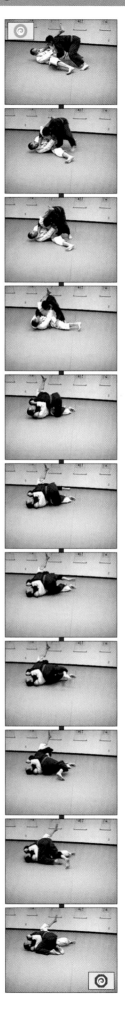

A similar pass can be done without attempting to stack the opponent's leg.

◀▶ After breaking the guard, Blue underhooks White's left leg with his right arm, and presses White's right knee to the mat with his left hand.

◀▶ Blue slides his left knee over the top of White's right thigh, as close to White's right hip as possible.

◀▶ Blue presses his weight forward and holds behind Blue's neck with his left hand. Maintaining the underhook with his right arm, Blue back steps over White's leg with his right foot, keeping his left foot hooked over White' right thigh for control.

◀▶ Blue scissors his left leg through below his right and establishes side control.

◀ Blue does not necessarily have to turn his hips. He can bring the trailing leg over White's right leg with his hips staying level. This variation is tighter.

Blue breaks White's guard with his right knee forward and presses White's right knee to the mat with his left palm (be sure to use your posture and weight to hold the leg down).

Keeping his weight forward, Blue begins to slide his right knee over the top of White's right thigh, as close to White's hip as possible.

As Blue's right knee touches the mat, he simultaneously lays his weight on top of White and swims his right hand under or posts it on the mat at White's left side. At the same time, Blue grabs White's right sleeve and lifts his arm to prevent White from pushing him away. At this point in the pass, you must lay your weight on top of your opponent's chest or he will push you off.

Pivoting on his right knee, Blue swings his left leg around under White's right armpit and comes into side control.

Sometimes when performing the pass on the preceding page - and indeed with a number of other passes - your opponent will attempt to stop you by catching your foot in a figure four leg hold.

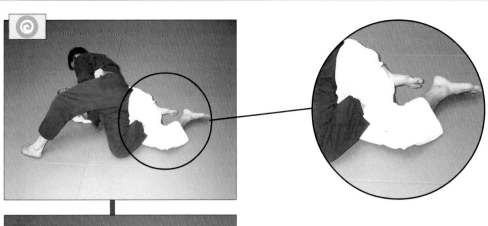

Blue pulls White's right arm up under his armpit to control his upper body, and smashes his weight onto White. This helps to immobilize White, if only briefly, while Blue frees his foot.

Posting his right knee on the mat for base, Blue places the sole of his free foot inside White's top knee.

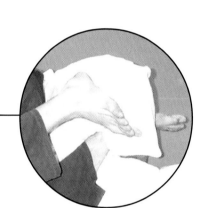

With his free foot Blue pushes back on the inside of White's knee as he simultaneously pulls his other foot free.

Blue twists his hips to the left, underhooks White's head with his left arm and comes to side control.

Sequence leading to this technique:
1. Blue tries to stack White's leg but White makes it too heavy to lift
2. Blue attempts to pass over White's other leg but White shifts his weight and blocks with his arm.
3. Now the opportunity to stack White presents itself.

Blue underhooks White's left leg with his right and pushes down on the inside of White's right leg with his left in an attempt to pass around to White's right side.

Blue lowers his weight and drops his left shoulder as he begins to pass around White's right side. White turns onto his right hip and pushes Blue back to stop the pass.

Now that White has committed his weight to his right side, Blue has an opportunity to stack White's left leg. Blue steps his right leg forward and at the same time changes direction. The forward momentum of Blue's right leg is key as it is transferred into the lifting and stacking action. Blue moves back around to his right and slides his right shoulder underneath White's left leg as he steps. Blue smashes his weight forward onto White.

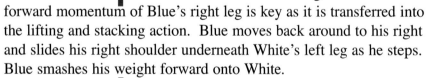

Blue moves around White's side and passes his Guard.

TOURNAMENT STRATEGY

In competition, there are several different strategies for passing the Guard. Important factors include the opponent and the circumstances. Following are some of the more common situations that occur, and some ideas on different strategies for dealing with the situations you may find yourself in. First we'll cover differences is size and physicality, and then different match situations.

Big vs. Small (heavy vs. light): When the opponent is larger and heavier than you, you will most likely have the advantage of speed. Very large opponents will usually not be able to move their hips as fast as smaller opponents.

If you can open the larger opponent's feet and control his legs, you will have a good chance to use speed to pass the Guard. It is important to try and keep your head up and avoid letting the opponent pull your head down to his chest. Fighters with strong arms will often be able to control your head and attack.

In the open Guard, stronger fighters will also be able to pull your arm in or head down for an armbar or Triangle choke. Maintaining proper base, allowing you to use the power of your legs is important for defense against a stronger opponent.

If you are heavier and stronger than your opponent, it is often easier to pass his Guard by

(CONT'D PG. 66)

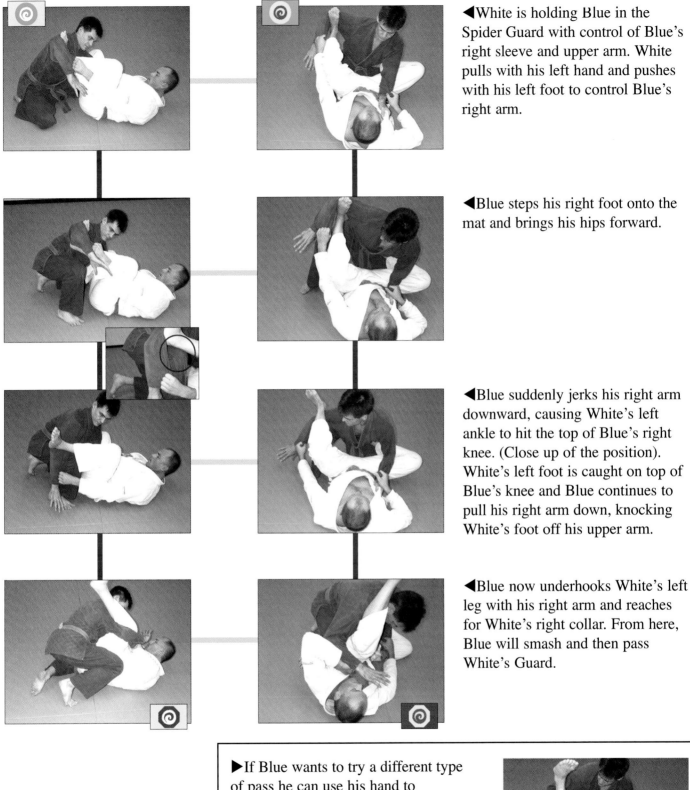

◀White is holding Blue in the Spider Guard with control of Blue's right sleeve and upper arm. White pulls with his left hand and pushes with his left foot to control Blue's right arm.

◀Blue steps his right foot onto the mat and brings his hips forward.

◀Blue suddenly jerks his right arm downward, causing White's left ankle to hit the top of Blue's right knee. (Close up of the position). White's left foot is caught on top of Blue's knee and Blue continues to pull his right arm down, knocking White's foot off his upper arm.

◀Blue now underhooks White's left leg with his right arm and reaches for White's right collar. From here, Blue will smash and then pass White's Guard.

▶If Blue wants to try a different type of pass he can use his hand to control White's leg after getting it off his elbow. Blue won't be able to control White's leg for long this way, but long enough for Blue to start whatever he wants to do next.

Blue breaks White's Guard and holds outside his hips with both hands.

Blue puts his right knee in the center of White's rear. He will use his thigh like a ramp to slide White's hips up.

Blue now locks his hands around White's thighs near his hips and pulls White's hips toward himself so that White slides up with his hips resting on top of Blue's right thigh.

Blue breaks the guard.

Blue lowers his torso and drops his elbows straight down inside White's legs.

Blue reaches his arms around the outsides of White's legs and hugs tightly.

ALTERNATE GRIPS FOR THE SMASH PASS

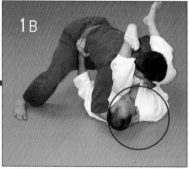

Blue smashes White and reaches behind his neck with his right arm.

Blue slips his right hand around the right side of White's neck to secure head control.

Blue can also grab over the top of White's right shoulder and lever his right forearm down across the front of White's throat (this grip is useful is White is not wearing a gi).

Blue sprawls his feet back and smashes White's knees toward his chest.

Blue grabs inside White's right collar with his right hand, thumb in (grab as deep inside the collar as possible).

Blue continues to smash White and circles around to White's left side to pass the Guard.

Keeping the tight hug around White's legs, Blues stands in base.

Using the power of his legs and hips, Blue pulls White into him and up, stacking White on the backs of his shoulders. Blue continues to hug tightly and squeezes inward with his knees against the outside of White's hips for control.

Sprawling his feet back for balance, Blue posts on the balls of his feet and pushes into White, smashing his weight downward. Blue reaches his left hand across White's body and grabs inside White's left lapel close to the neck, with his thumb in. At the same time, Blue grabs the back of White's belt.

Blue shuffles his feet around to his left, lifts on White's belt and smashes his weight onto White with the intent of crushing White's knees into his face.

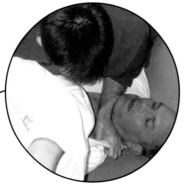

It is also important to crush across the top of the opponent's throat with your left wrist.

White's legs will fall to his side and Blue pass the guard to side control.

DEALING WITH A STIFF ARM DEFENSE

During the double underhooks pass, White counters by pushing Blue's hip with his arm.

Blue maintains the smashing pressure and brings his left knee over the top of White's elbow.

Blue drops his weight over his forward knee, forcing White's blocking arm to bend. Blue can now complete the pass.

White attempts to stop Blue by pushing his hip away.

Blue slides his knee up inside of White's arm.

Blue drops his weight onto his left knee, smashing White's right arm to the ground. From here, Blue can complete the smash pass.

METHODS FOR HOLDING AN OPPONENT IN A STACKED POSITION

Hold the belt.

Hold the top of the pants.

Hold the wrist and brace with the knee.

Blue holds White's right lapel with his right hand, and brings his hips up close to White. He lets go of White's belt with his left hand and reaches underneath White's hips to grab his right wrist.

◀... Blue focuses his weight onto his forearm and affects a choke from side control. He could also do the move from the balls of his feet to increase the pressure.

Blue maintains his grip (*here he has switched to a sleeve grip*). White cannot role forward due to Blue's fore-arm positioned across his throat. Blue pulls White's right wrist up behing his back, chicken-wing style.

◀... Blue sits on his right hip as he scissors his right leg through. Blue puts his left foot on the top of White's left hip for control, and simultaneously pulls up on White's right arm as he pushes down on White's left hip for a shoulder lock submission.

This is a very bad position for White. White is pinned and several submis-sions are avail-able to Blue...

❂ In these variations, Blue pulls White's arm behind his back to clear the way for the pass and set up a mount or submission from side control. The key is getting the grip on the hand opposite the side of which you are passing. This works well with the double underhook pass or the smash pass at the beginning of this chapter.

◀... If White stays on his side Blue can submit him via the shoul-der by push-ing his wrist toward the mat. This will only work if White's arm is bent at the elbow.

Blue sets up the double underhook smash and pass, but White attempts to stop him by hooking his feet inside Blue's knees. With White's hooks in place, Blue is unable to lift and stack White on his shoulders.

Blue slides his right knee back to clear White's hook. Pressure from Blue's right forearm blocks White's leg from following Blue's leg.

Blue moves his knee back and to the inside of White's left leg. This will keep White from reinserting his leg as in the first picture.

Continuing, Blue keeps hugging White's legs tightly and slides his left leg back to clear White's right hook.

▲Unobstruced view of the correct body position when clearing the hooks: Keeping the hips down, slide one leg straight back to clear the hook, then slide the knee up inside the opponent's leg until your knee and elbow are together, leaving **no space** for the opponent to put a hook back in.

❷ Hiding the elbow inside the knee is useful in a number of situations. It nullifies a number of arm attacks from the guard.

Blue now slides his left knee back up inside White's right leg. Blue is now free of White's hooks. How he can resume his pass.

Blue breaks the guard open or perhaps White opens up to attack.

Blue moves forward closing up the space between his body and White's, while maintaining his grip on White's hips. Blue keeps his elbows locked down tightly.

This is not the smashing guard pass seen at the beginning of this chapter. The idea here is to rotate around the leg.

This is a close up of Blue's position from the other side. Blue has dropped his right elbow down to the mat, and is laying his weight over White's left knee. Blue locks his right elbow down tightly and maintains his grip on White's hip. It is extremely important to control White's left leg to avoid the triangle choke.

Keeping his weight down, blue reaches back with his left and inserts the hand through the space behind White's knee.

Blue pushes his chest forward and reaches his left hand across White's chest.

This technique is not about smashing White as shown previously. Rather, it is about controlling the leg and spinning around.

Blue grabs inside White's left collar, holding with the thumb in. Blue sprawls back onto the balls of his feet.

Blue shuffles his feet around to his left. He maintains some pressure with his shoulder all the while. Blue twists his head to the right a little, looking away and pressing his left shoulder downward.

Blue clears White's leg and establishes side control.

White's guard is open.

White puts his right knee on Blue's chest. From here White is in a position to attack. Blue does not want that.

Blue pushes White's right knee down and keeps it down with weight from his chest.

Blue grabs White's left arm with his right ...

... and sprawls his feet back, laying the weight of his upper body on White's legs.

Pulling White's left thigh back, Blue shuffles his feet around to his right, keeping his weight low and on the balls of his feet.

From White's scissors attack position, Blue reaches between White's legs and holds with his palm over the top of White's right thigh.

Blue sprawls back and smashes his weight onto White's knees. Notice how he keeps his head down and pressing into White's hips.
Blue grabs White's right arm with his left for control.

Keeping his weight down, Blue begins to shuffle his feet around to his left.

Here it is from another angle.

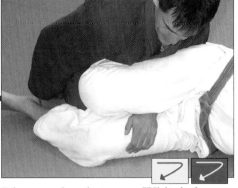

Blue reaches between White's legs with his left hand (inserting his hand from behind White's top leg) and grabs over the top of White's left thigh with his palm.
[*See sidebar.*]

As soon as he clears White's legs, Blue slides his left knee up against White's left hip.

Blue underhooks White's head and establishes side control.

Blue clears White's legs and immediately brings his right knee up to block White's right hip.

Blue drives forward to side control.

RE: GRIPPING

This is an example of a bad grip on the leg. White is grabbing the cloth instead of over the top of the thigh.

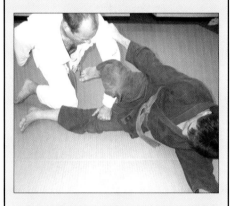

Because of the slack in the cloth, Blue is able to extend his right leg ...

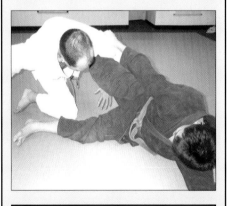

... and snap off White's grip.

Blue attempts to pass the scissors position. Defending, White brings his top knee up high to block the pass.

Keeping his hips and weight down, Blue turns his left hand palm upward (Blue's left hand was holding over the top of White's left thigh) and grabs around the front of White's top (right) thigh.

Because White's top leg is blocking Blue, Blue must get it out of the way.

From the other side: Blue attempts to pass the scissors position, but White brings his top leg high to block.

Blue changes his grip to a palm up hold on the top of White's left thigh.

Blue lifts his hips a little, and pulls White's left leg back out of the way.

Blue slides his right knee in and passes the guard.

Keeping his head and chest down, Blue lifts his hips slightly and pulls White's right thigh back to clear the leg.

As soon as Blue pulls White's top leg back and out of the way, he brings his left knee up against White's left hip.

Blue underhooks White's head and comes to side control.

▼Once Blue slips in his left knee, White no longer has space to replace the guard.

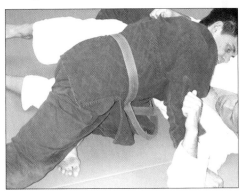

IF YOUR OPPONENT PUSHES UP...

  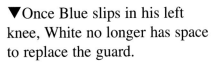

Blue is attempting to pass the scissors position, but White pushes his upper body away, preventing him from putting his weight down to pass.

Blue turns his hips so that he leads with his left as White pushes his chest up.

Blue takes advantage of the space and slides his left knee across White's hips for the knee on belly position. Blue adjusts his base.

◉ Timing is key. Blue's jump must coincide with the White player attempting to bring his bottom leg under to fix his position.

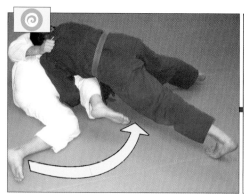

Once again Blue attempts to pass the scissors position. This time, however, White will defend against Blue pulling back his top leg. As Blue pulls ...

... White attempts to twist his hips and bring his bottom leg through and put Blue back into the guard. As on the preceding page, Blue has changed his left grip to hold White's top leg and has pulled it back to make space to pass.

Because White is countering by bringing his low leg back through, Blue uses the moment to reverse his direction of attack. Keeping the weight of his upper body down, he jumps over White's legs to his rear. He keeps his left shoulder and head pushing down on White's hips as he springs over. This keeps White from hooking his to leg into Blue's legs. Also, a bit of height on the jump makes a big difference.

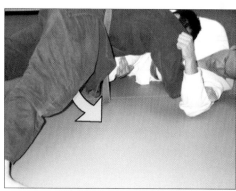

Here is a view form the other side. Note the placement of Blues hands.

This move requires sensitivity to White's movement. As white tries to bring his bottom leg under to stop the pass (pictured) Blue must simlutaneously spring himself the other way.

This pass requires little strength, but a measure of agility.

Blue lands in a sprawl position behind White.

Blue has control of White's low arm so it is unlikely he will easily be able to turn to his knees. Blue moves up toward White's head and applies weight with his chest.

Blue lets go of the leg and uses it control White's head.

From here Blue has all but completed the pass.

Blue attempts to pass the scissors position, but White pushes his hips away and scissors his legs, breaking Blue's grip on his left leg.

Blue quickly switches his left grip to hold over White' right knee. Blue then switches his hips. He posts off his left foot and scissors his right foot under him, trapping over White's right ankle with his own right ankle.

This is the position in the previous picture from another angle. Notice how Blue keeps his hips low.

▲▼ The same pass from different viewing angles. While Blue attempts to pass the scissors position, White pushes him away and scissors his legs, breaking Blue's grip.

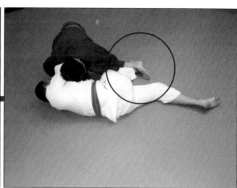

▲▼ Blue grabs over the top of White's right leg, drops his right hip to the mat and scissors his right foot through, pressing his right ankle over the top of White's right ankle.

Continuing, Blue swings his left leg over White's hips, putting his knee down behind White while simultaneously hugging over White's back with his left arm. Blue hugs White tightly with his arms and legs. Notice that Blue's right leg is still trapping White's right ankle.

Blue slides his weight over White's hips and moves to his rear, still hugging tightly.

Blue swings his right leg to White's rear, establishing side control.

▲▼ Blue swings his left foot over White, while smashing his weight down.

▲▼ Blue hugs White tightly with his left arm as he shifts his weight over the top of White's hips, putting his left knee down behind White.

▲ Blue swings his right leg over to White's rear, and comes to side control.

▼ To keep White from going to his knees, Blue must keep good control. Here Blue hugs the head and arm.

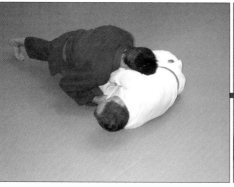

While attempting to pass the scissors position, White defends by pushing Blue away and bringing his right knee up to block Blue's hips.

Keeping his weight down, Blue hooks his left arm over the top of White's right knee and pulls his leg down.

Blue hooks his left leg over the top of White's right leg, hooking behind his knee.

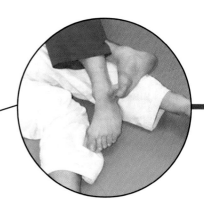

This is a variation of the pass above. Blue hooks his left leg over White's right leg.

After Blue hooks his left foot over White's right leg, he hooks his right ankle over the top of White's right ankle, pinning it to the floor.

 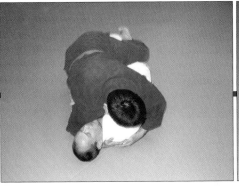 

White attempts to pull his right leg free. The result is that White begins to pull Blue toward the mount. Blue begins to move up toward White's head.

Blue underhooks White' head with his right arm for control...

... and comes to top mount.

 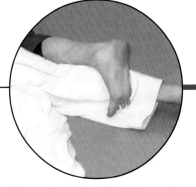 

Since White has his right leg crossed over his left, pinning White's right leg down effectively pins both of his legs.

Blue drops his left hip and moves toward White's rear. Notice that Blue has switched his right grip to hold White's right knee, keeping his leg under control.

▶Blue is in an ideal position for attack.

Another variation on passing the scissors position. Blue has begun the pass and has moved up toward White's head. White defends by pushing Blue's hips away, preventing him from moving his hips in for side control.

Blue ducks his head down and posts the top of his head on the mat in front of White's chest.

Posting off his head, Blue kicks his feet up and over White.

Again, Blue attempts to pass the scissors position. White defends by pushing his hip away.

Blue ducks his head and posts the top of his head in front of White's chest.

Maintaining his grips, Blue kicks his feet up and over White.

Maintaining his grips, Blue lands in the bridge position over White.

Blue keeps his weight on top of White, releases his left grip, twists his hips to the right and scissors his right leg through to the rear.

Blue establishes side control.

▲Blue establishes side control by underhooking White's head. Blue needs to use his weight to keep White from going to his knees.

Blue lands in a bridge over White.

Blue releases his left grip, and begins to turn toward his right.

▲Here Blue traps White's right arm. This method provides greater control because White is blocked from rolling to his stomach as his arm is trapped.

White turns onto his right side and slides his left shin across Blue's hips in the scissors sweep position.
Maintaining his grip, Blue moves his hips back a little and lowers his weight

Keeping his hold on White's hip with his left hand, Blue reaches behind White's left ankle with his right hand.

Blue reaches up and grabs White's belt, trapping White' left foot against his rear.

This is the same pass from another angle, Blue hooks behind White's left ankle with his right hand.

Blue grabs the back of White's belt, locking his foot to his rear.

Blue lays his chest on top of White's legs, pinning them to the mat.

Blue lays his chest over the top of White's left leg, smashing White' legs down against the mat.

Keeping his weight on top of White's legs, Blue sprawls his feet back, posting on the balls of his feet.

Blue shuffles his feet around to his left, clearing White's legs. Blue then reaches behind White's neck and moves his right knee against White's right hip, coming to side control.

Blue sprawls his feet back, keeping his weight on White's legs. Blue shuffles his feet to his left ...

... and passes the guard.

For every move there is a counter.

By way of example we review the scissors pass series.

Once Blue gets his pass started, there are a number of ways White might react. Rather then insisting on one technique, Blue works around White's defenses, nullifying them and using them to his own advantage.

Applying force directly against force has its place, but does not make for good technique.

Using what an opponent gives you is fundamental to good Jiu-Jitsu, Judo, and grappling.

White tries a scissors sweep; Blue flattens White's leg and comes around.

White defends with his top leg; Blue pulls it back.

White straight arms and pushes up; Blue goes knee in belly.

White shoots his bottom leg through as Blue pulls on the top leg; Blue jumps over.

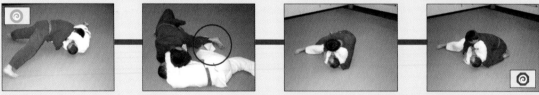

White straight arms Blue and pushes low; Blue steps over the shin.

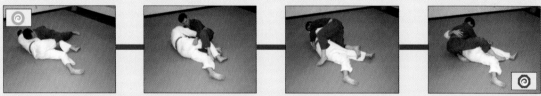

White straight arms Blue; Blue climbs over the leg.

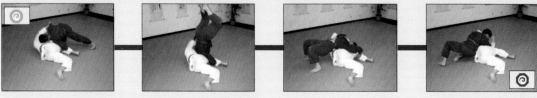

White pushes into Blue's hips; Blue flips over.

Blue holds inside White's right leg with his left hand, grabbing the cloth thumb down.

Blue lowers his torso and rolls his right arm underneath White's left leg. It is important to lower the body as you wrap the arm in order to hold the opponent's leg close to your shoulder.

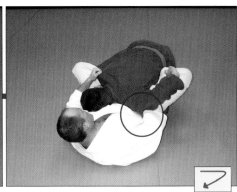

Blue pushes down with his left arm, turns his head to the right and smashes his left shoulder into White's hips.

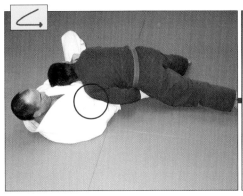

Blue shuffles his feet moving around White's legs to his left. As you shuffle the feet, do not take the forward pressure off of White's hips, and the feet should not cross.

Once Blue had cleared White's right leg, he grabs White's right leg cloth with his right hand and drives his right knee up against White's right hip.

Blue underhooks White's head with his left arm and establishes side control.

This time Blue goes the other direction. He sprawls both legs back and uses his upper body to smash White's left leg to the mat.

Be sure the hips press toward the mat.

Keeping his weight down, Blue shuffles his feet moving around to White's left, as he pushes White's left leg the opposite way.

Blue quickly slides his left knee up against White's left hip and reaches up with his right arm to control White's head.

Blue slides his right knee up and holds side control.

Blue has opened White's guard.

Blue brings his leg around so that his knee is positioned in contact with White's foot.

Blue slides his leg back so that his leg pins White's heel against White's butt.

Keeping his weight down, Blue grabs the cloth *underneath* White's left leg, and inserts his left arm below White's right knee from the inside, hugging White's right leg.

Blue leans his weight forward onto White's left leg, holding tightly with his arms so that White cannot move his left leg or hips. Blue begins to slide his right leg back, keeping his center of gravity low.

Keeping his weight on top of White's left leg, Blue swings his left foot back over his right, with his feet wide for stability.

Holding White's right leg tightly, Blue steps his right leg back under his left.

Next he reaches under White's neck with his right arm to control White's head and quickly slides his left knee up against White's left hip, passing his guard to side control.

◀ Be careful about leaving your arm between your opponents legs anytime you pass. There is a danger that he will push your head toward his feet and throw on a reverse triangle choke with his legs.

The same technique viewed from the front. Blue moves his right leg back and over the top of White's right ankle.

Blue slides his right leg up to trap White's right foot close to his butt.

Blue grabs the cloth under White's right leg and inserts his left arm around White's right leg. *He could also post the hand on the mat.*

Blue leans forward to smash White's leg to the mat.

Blue leans his weight onto White's leg and pins it to the mat. Turning his head to the left, Blue lays his weight onto White and slides his right foot back.

Keeping his weight down, Blue swings his left foot back over his right.

Blue scissors his right leg through from below his left.

Blue hugs White's head as he moves his left knee into White's left hip for side control.

This pass begins like the preceding one. It is shown from two angles.

Blue traps White's left foot and gets his grip. He uses his left arm to keep White from bring his leg across his body.

Blue sprawls both feet back, smashing his upper body weight onto White's left leg.

Turning his head to the left and using his right shoulder to post on White's left hip. Blue presses the mat with his left foot and swings his right foot upward followed by the left foot as his hips come straight up.

Blue uses the momentum from his legs to hop over. He continues to press down onto White's left hip. Blue cannot afford to be gentle. He must bring his full weight to bear on his shoulder and into White's stomach. He must commit to the pass.

Blue turns his hips to the left while in the air, and lands on White's left side in side control, his knees close to White's hip and armpit.

Blue is attempting to pass White's Open Guard around White's left side. Blue has control of White's left leg, and White is pushing Blue away with his **arms locked out at the elbows**.

Blue suddenly twists his body to the left, drops his right hip into White and swings his left foot over as he reaches his left arm around toward White's head.

Blue lays back onto White, hugging around White's right side with his left arm.

Blue continues spinning to his left, steps his right leg over his left and drops on his knees for side control.

BREAKING DOWN STRAIGHT ARMS

White blocks Blue from coming to his side by locking his arms out at the elbows.

Blue snaps his hip into White's wrists. White has to bend at the elbows or his writs will be painfully jammed. Once White bends his elbows it becomes very difficult for him to resist Blue's pressure.

Once White's elbows bend Blue can:

1. Drop directly down on White; or

2. Spin.

1 Blue opens White's guard.

2 Blue hooks his right thigh over the top of White's left foot.

3 Blue slides his right leg up, pinning White's left heel to his rear.

4 Keeping his weigh pressing forward, Blue slides his left leg back.

5 Blue then slides his left knee up to trap the top of White's left ankle. The top of White's left foot is trapped outside Blue's left hip.

6 Blue grips the top of White's left leg with his right hand and underhooks White's right leg with his left.

7 Blue looks to his left, sprawls his legs back and smashes his weight on top of White's hips and inside left thigh.

8 Keeping the same grip, Blue steps his left foot back over his right.

9 Blue scissors his right leg through, and reaches behind White's head with his right hand.

10 Blue drives forward to establish side control.

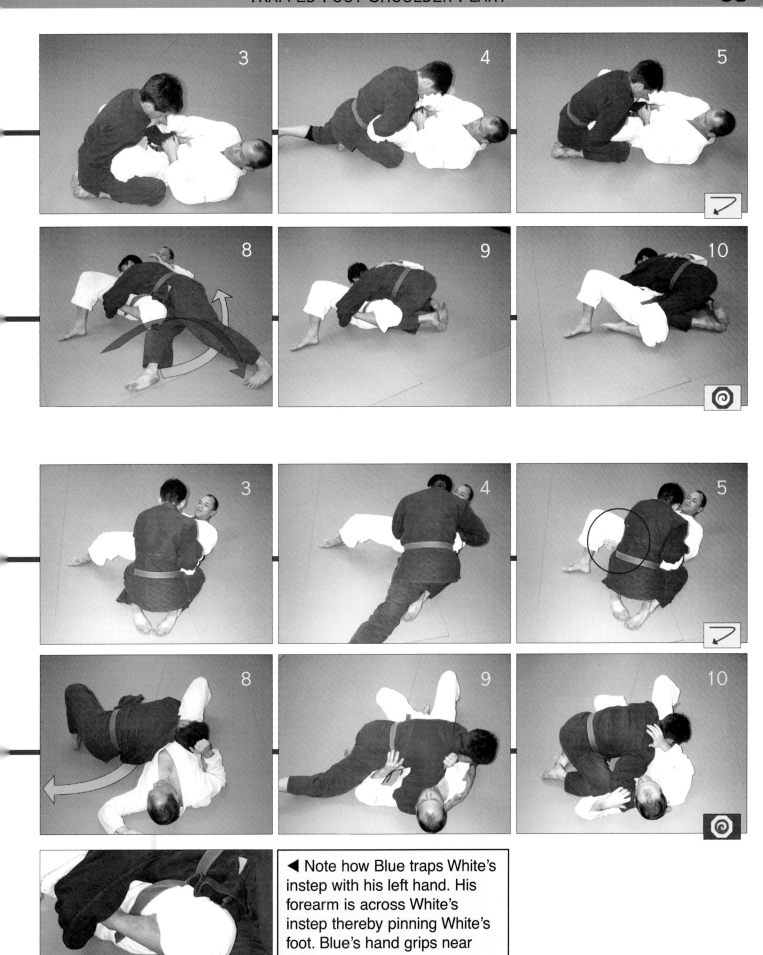

◄ Note how Blue traps White's instep with his left hand. His forearm is across White's instep thereby pinning White's foot. Blue's hand grips near White's hip or butt.

Blue is in White's Open Guard. Blue posts his left palm on the mat between White's legs. With his right hand, Blue grabs inside White's left knee, grabbing the cloth thumb down.

Blue lays his right shoulder down on top of White's hips, and turns his head to the left. Blue posts on the balls of his feet.

Pushing off with his right foot, Blue swings his left leg straight up to his rear.

Blue lands in a bridge, feet on the opposite of his head.

Blue twists his body to the left letting go of White's leg and slides his right foot back for base. Blue puts his left arm down on the mat at White's right side.

HEAD BETWEEN LEGS VARIATION

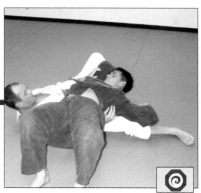

This is a variation of the technique shown above. The technique is the same except Blue puts his head down in between White's legs instead of posting his shoulder on White's hips.

As his left foot goes vertical, Blue follows by swinging his right foot up beside his left.

Blue lands in a bridge, feet on the opposite of his head.

Blue scissors his left leg back under his right and underhooks White's head with his right arm, establishing side control.

Maintaining his grip on White's left leg with his right hand, Blue turns over kicking his left foot over his right and posting his left hand outside White's right side.

Blue lets go of White's leg with his right, and underhooks White's head for side control.

Blue attempts to hug White's legs and pass the Guard. Here Blue is moving around to his right side, but White stops the pass by pushing against Blue's back.

Blue swings his left leg over White's legs and locks his feet below White's ankles.

Blue lowers his hips, hugging tightly with his arms and legs. Blue keeps his hips pressed low to the ground. His ankles are crossed, trapping White's legs.

As White attempts to push Blue down, Blue will slowly inch his way up White's body (as if climbing a tree). Blue keeps White's knees close together until he clears them.

Blue works his way up to the top mount.

CHAPTER 3

STANDING GUARD PASSES

Besides breaking and passing the Guard on the knees, the other option is to stand and pass the Guard. As with passing on the knees, there are relative advantages and disadvantages to the standing passes. In general, passing the Guard while standing allows the fighter to use the advantage of speed over strength. Very often the smaller and lighter fighter will find it easier to pass the Guard standing. It is sometimes easier to break a very tight Closed Guard by standing first. Standing results in the opponent's hips being lifted off the mat, negating much of the power and mobility they have with their hips down. With the opponent hanging from your hips in the Closed Guard as you stand, gravity is on your side as your opponent must use considerable energy just to hang on with his legs. Very often pressing down on the inside of the opponent's knees or wedging a knee in between his legs will be sufficient to break the Guard. The downside of standing to break a Closed Guard is that you are left more vulnerable to sweeps as your center of gravity is higher and your base is smaller than on the knees.

Although standing to pass the Guard allows you to use speed to your advantage, it also generally requires more energy expenditure than passes from the knees. The advantage to the freedom of movement standing affords is the potential to build up considerable momentum. You can build momentum in your own movements (side to side for example) and pass with speed, or you can build up momentum to move or control the opponent's legs as you pass. When standing, the possibility of jumping or cartwheeling passes also arises.

Most of the submissions available from the Guard are also available when you are standing.

Your vulnerability to sweeps is, however, typically higher when standing to pass. When standing, your center of gravity is higher and your base smaller. The opponent basically has two categories of sweep available. First, the opponent grabs or blocks your ankles or feet, attempting to trip you backward. Second, the opponent has control of your arms or upper body and his foot or feet in your hips. Here there is the possibility of being swept sideways or head first in a roll.

As you pass the Guard, it is important to constantly pay attention to the positioning of the opponents hands, feet, and hips, so that you can adjust your position and reduce or eliminate the potential of being swept. While standing, you are also vulnerable to the opponent's Spider Guard (his feet in your biceps as he pulls on your sleeves) or De La Riva position (the opponent's leg wrapped around the outside of your leg and inserted between your legs from the rear).

Other possible dangers while standing are foot locks, knee bars, and heel hooks. All are more easily set up by your opponent when you are standing. You must be on guard against leg submissions if the opponent threads his leg around yours from between your legs, or if he begins to turn and trap your leg between his legs. Footlocks are also set up if the opponent trips you backward onto the mat. On the other hand, you too have many opportunities to attack the opponent's legs as you pass the Guard standing. These techniques are covered later in Chapters 4 & 5. One final catogory of attack to guard against is the potential for the opponent to quickly go to his knees and shoot for a single or double leg takedown.

Obviously you need to stand before you can do a standing pass. Here are ways to do so.

Blue holds White under his armpits.

Keeping his head up, his back straight and his hips down, Blue lifts his left knee and puts his left foot on the mat. Blue places his foot down far enough back that White cannot grab his ankle.

Blue lifts his right knee and comes to the squat position. Blue keeps his hips low, his head up and his back straight.

Blue straightens his legs and lifts White's hips off the ground. Blue pinches White's hips between his knees for control.

A variation on standing up in the guard. Blue sits in base and holds at White's armpits.

Blue lifts his head and hips up, while holding White. Blue keeps his head up and his back straight.

Blue pops up in one smooth motion, both legs at once. Blue uses his fists for balance and base.

You can pop off your toes (*above*) or from your insteps (*below*).

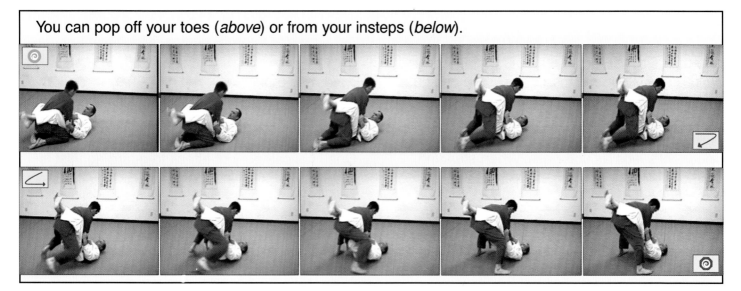

This one works better without the gi because there is less for the bottom player to hold onto.

After standing, Blue thrusts his hips forward as he leans backward slightly. The forward pressure of the hips breaks White's guard open. The movement should be done explosively

STANDING CAN OPENER

Blue holds behind White's head with both hands. Hold the back of the head, not behind the neck. Blue pinches the outsides of White's hips with his knees as he pulls White's head forward and downward, trying to touch White's chin to his chest. At the same time, Blue squats and pushes forward with his hips. The pressure on the back of White's neck causes him to open his feet.

◀ Blue stands in White's Closed Guard and grabs his lapels with four fingers in each side.

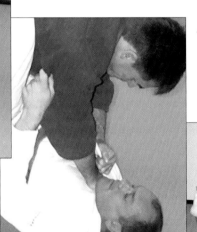

◀ Blue pushes his right fist across White's throat. Blue pulls the cloth over his right fist with his left hand.

◀ Close up of the grip.

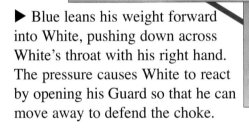

▶ Blue leans his weight forward into White, pushing down across White's throat with his right hand. The pressure causes White to react by opening his Guard so that he can move away to defend the choke.

In this variation, Blue stands in White's Closed Guard and grabs inside the lapels fingers in and thumbs up. There must not be any slack in the gi.

Blue pushes both fists into the sides of White's neck by rolling his big knuckles in. His knuckles go from pointing at each other to the ground.

ATTACK

> ⊘ When you are standing and have opened the guard you must beware of ankle sweeps.

White stands in Blue's Guard to begin his pass.

Blue grabs behind both of White's ankles, as close to White's heels as possible.

Blue slides his hips forward underneath White. He pinches his knees together.

Holding White's feet, Blue pushes with his legs to sweep White onto his butt. Blue keeps his hips on the mat during the push. As White begins to fall, Blue sits up.

Blue quickly grabs White's lapel with his left hand so that he can pull himself up to the mount.

Blue bends his left leg back, and pulls himself up to the mount.

COUNTER

As White attempts to sweep Blue, Blue grabs both of White's lapels and pulls himself down to counter the backwards push of the sweep.

Blue stands up in White's closed guard.

Keeping his back straight, Blue squats and stands up straight. White will not release his grip, and is lifted off the mat.

Blue puts his right palm inside of White's left knee.

Blue pushes down on the inside of White's knee and bounces up and down rapidly to shake White's feet open.

Blue stands in the closed guard. White hangs on and is lifted off the mat.

Blue pushes down on the inside of White's left knee.

White begins to slide down Blue's legs.

In this variation, Blue stands in the guard.

Glue feels which leg is on top and orks that one. Blue reaches back with his right hand.

He inserts his right hand between White's ankles.

Blue hooks his right hand underneath White's left ankle.

As White hits the ground, Blue drops on top of him and passes his right knee over White's left thigh. At the same time Blue hugs behind White's head.

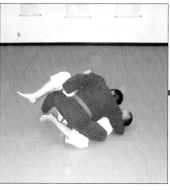

Blue underhooks White's right leg with his left arm.

Keeping his right foot hooked over the top of White's left thigh, blue steps his left foot back out of the guard.

Posting on his left foot, Blue scissors his right leg through and establishes side control.

Blue pushes White down to the mat, but White keeps his feet locked.

Blue pins White's left leg to the mat, turns his hips to the right and slides both knees over the top of White's legs.

Blue slides down to the mat and pulls up on White's left sleeve, sliding his left hand under White's right armpit, coming to the modified scarf hold position.

Blue bends forward, pushing White down to the mat with his left hand and prying White's guard open with his right arm.

Continuing, Blue twists his hips to his right, drops his right knee and reaches his right hand across to grab White's right collar with the thumb in and...

...smashes his weight down on top of White. Blue twists to his right and smashes his right hip and shoulder into White, pressing White's knee into his head.

White gets uncomfortable and takes his leg off Blue's head. Blue passes the guard.

Blue stands in the guard.

Blue twists his hips, pressing his knee into White's ribs. The pressure breaks White's feet open.

Keeping the pressure on, Blue maintains his right grip inside White's left knee and reaches under White's right leg with his left hand. Blue uses the back of his hand to slide under White's leg.

> ❷ These techniques work well in combination with each other.

In this variation of the pass above, as Blue attempts to come around to White's right side, White pushes Blue's hip away to stop the pass.

Maintaining his hold on White's left collar with his left hand, Blue smashes his weight straight down.

Keeping his weight down, Blue reaches his right arm behind White's neck.

Blue drops his weight down and smashes White. Blue reaches his left hand across to grab thumb inside White's left collar.

Blue sprawls his left leg back, smashing White's left knee into his head.

Blue turns his head to the right and White's right leg slips over. Blue comes to side control.

Blue slides his right knee over the top of White's left thigh.

Blue drops his right knee to the mat, and keeping his right foot hooked over the top of White's left leg, Blue steps his left foot back over White's left leg.

Posting on his left foot, Blue scissors his right leg through, coming to side control.

◉ Some passes can be done either tight and slow or fast and loose. Below is a video sequence demonstrating the fast and loose version of the pass shown above. [*The pictures below show Blue going to the opposite way from those above.*] An effective ploy is to switch from a methodical pass to one relying on quickness, without warning.

Blue is in White's closed Guard. Blue grips White's lapel and inside his leg.

Blue stands, but White keeps his Guard closed.

Blue switches his grips to the tops of White's hips and bounces up and down rapidly as he pushes down on White's hipbone with his hand.

White's feet open and he slides back down to the mat. Blue squats over White's hips and sits his weight down, preparing to pass. It is important that Blue squeeze White's knees together at this point. Doing so helps to briefly immobilize Blue's legs.

TOURNAMENT STRATEGY
(CONT'D FROM PG. 24)

smashing him with your body weight. You will also be able to maintain strong grips and holds as you pass. With a good base, it will be harder for the smaller fighter to sweep you as you pass.

Tall vs. Short: When fighting a taller fighter, especially one with long legs, it is important to watch for armbar and triangle choke techniques. In general, it is also more difficult to break open the feet of taller fighters. Taller fighters are usually at a disadvantage when you smash their legs into their chests or over their heads.

If your opponent is shorter than you, passing under the legs is generally more difficult. Techniques that involve passing over or around the legs of shorter fighters are often easier to apply.

More Flexible vs. Less Flexible: Generally speaking, the opponent who is more flexible will have more options for attack and defense from his Guard. A very flexible Guard can be extremely difficult to pass. If you can limit the mobility of the opponent's hips, you will have a better chance of passing. Playing a tight game, staying close to the opponent's hips and keeping your weight crushing him will often prove useful against flexible opponents.

Inflexible opponents have difficulty with being smashed. They tend to find folded positions quite uncomfortable and will give up sidecontrol rather than test the limits of their flexibility. This is also true of players with large bellies.

Blue is caught in the Spider Guard.

Blue drops his left knee to the mat for base.

Blue pulls his right arm down sharply and causes White's left calf to strike against Blue's right knee, this frees one arm (White's left foot slips off Blue's biceps).

Blue reaches his right arm around White's left leg and grabs White's right lapel for control.

Blue now turns his body to the right and presses his left knee behind White's right knee, pushing White's foot off his left biceps.

Blue drops his weight and is free to continue passing the Guard.

Tight and Slow vs. Fast and Loose: One's overall Jiu Jitsu game can be divided into tight and slow or fast and loose. The strategy for which type of game you play is determined much the same as the strategy for fighting heavier or lighter opponent's. When you are heavier and stronger than your opponent, a slower, tighter game work well. When your opponent is heavier and stronger than you, a faster game may be better.

Conclusion: It is apparent from the above examples that it is best to develop a well rounded strategy and variety of techniques to deal with different sized fighters with different strategies. Obviously, the ability to change with circumstances and apply your strengths against your opponent's weaknesses is a hallmark of proper application of strategy.

You cannot pass if your opponent has control of your body with his feet. Once you break his contact, pass.

MOVE BACKWARD

Blue stands in White's open guard. White grips Blue's upper body and puts both feet on Blue's hips.

Blue grabs inside White's knees with both hands, gripping with the thumbs angled back toward himself.

Blue jumps his feet back into a sprawl position, pushing down on White's legs with his body weight. From here, Blue can begin to pass around White's legs.

MOVE FORWARD

White grips Blue's lapel and puts both feet on Blue's shoulders.

Blue lowers his hips a little for balance and grabs below White's ankles with the palms up.

Blue straightens his body and moves his hips forward. He leans back slightly as he pushes White's feet up above his head.

MOVE TO THE SIDE

White has both feet on Blue's hips. Blue grabs inside White's knees.
Blue reaches his right arm around the outside of White's left ankle, and grabs across underneath

Blue reaches his left hand across and grabs inside White's left knee.
Turning his hips to the left, Blue pulls White's legs to his right, clearing the feet.

White grabs Blue's sleeves and puts his feet on Blue's biceps. By pulling on the sleeves and pushing on the biceps, White controls Blue's arms and upper body movement.

Blue lowers his hips for balance and circles his hands up and inside of White's lower legs.

Blue continues, pushing his hands forward lifting White's hips off the ground.

Blue turns his palms over, and grabs the cloth inside White's knees.

Blue drives his weight forward, and smashes White's right leg toward his face. Notice Blue has circled his left elbow underneath White's right knee.

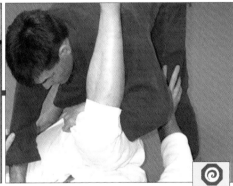

Close up of Blue's left arm position, with the elbow under White's knee for leverage. From this position, Blue can pass around White's right side.

White pushes Blue's right hip with his left foot, and pulls Blue's left sleeve with his right arm, right foot pushing the biceps.

To clear White's left foot, Blue lowers his body and circles his right elbow inside White's left knee.

Blue now closes his right knee up to his right elbow, forming a barrier so that White cannot put his left foot back on the hip or biceps. At the same time, Blue moves his left leg up to press behind White's right leg.

Blue lowers his hips and presses his weight through his left knee, pushing White's right knee toward his own chest, clearing the foot on the biceps.

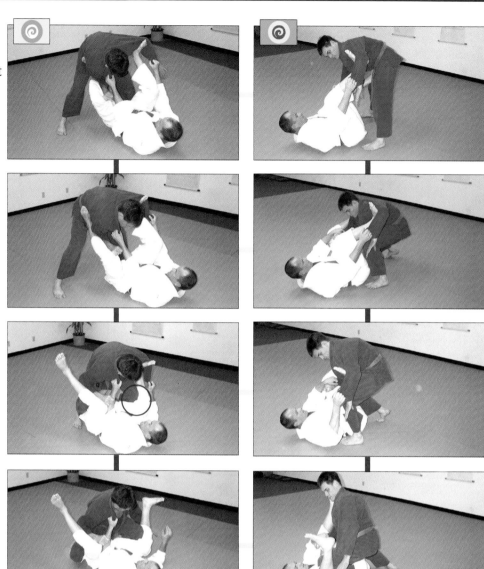

White is pushing Blue's left biceps with his right foot and pulling the sleeve down with his hand.

Blue puts his foot on the inside of White's right knee.

Blue steps his foot down, pushing White's right leg to the mat and freeing his arm.

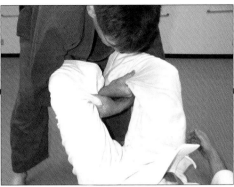

White puts both feet on Blue's hips.

Blue reaches around the outsides of White's legs and grabs the cloth near the knees on both sides.

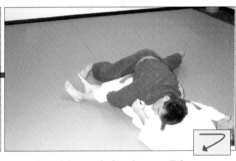

Blue pulls out with his elbows, squeezing White's legs together.

Blue sprawls back and lays his weight on top of White's legs, turning his head to look to the side.

Keeping his weight down, Blue begins to shuffle his feet around to his left. Blue moves around until he clears White's feet.

Blue moves his right hand over to underhook White's right hip, and then reaches for head control with his left arm to establish side control.

This technique works even when the opponent has a firm grip on both your sleeves. In other words, it can be done without first breaking his grip.

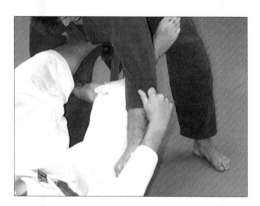

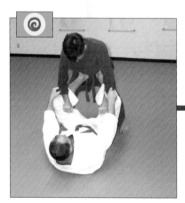   

White has his feet on Blue's hips and has a grip on Blue's sleeves.

Blue lowers his base, grabs White's right sleeve and reaches around the outside of White's leg with his right arm.

Blue grabs cloth near White's knee. At the same time, Blue grabs White's right sleeve with his left hand.

Blue steps back with his left foot to help clear White's leg from Blue's left hip. As soon as he has made a little space he begins pulling White's legs to the side.

❂ Make sure to pull his legs across your front at the same time you move your hips back.

❂ The path of Blue's hands is as if he was drawing an arch or turning a big wheel.

Blue steps back with his right foot to clear his right hip, and begins to pull White's left hand toward him as he pushes White's feet away from him. Blue thrusts his right arm away from himself in an archlike motion. He wants to spin White 90 degrees, pivoting him on the curve of his back.

Blue continues to pull White's sleeve toward him (Blue) as he pushes the legs away. This causes White to spin in place, and makes space for Blue to pass the Guard.

Once Blue has cleared White's feet, he immediately steps up with his right foot, to the knee on belly position. Notice Blue still has control of White's legs and arm.

◀ Blue grips White's wrist and knee and puts his left knee on belly.

Somethimes you will not be able to get the rear knee in the belly. In trying to defend you from doing so, your opponent may leave an opening for the front knee. This technique exploits those situations.

◀ Blue pushes off his right foot, driving his weight into White as he slides his shin across White's hips.

◀ Blue releases his right grip and spins his body to his right, swinging his right leg back over White's head.

Drill the spin part until you can make the turn smoothly. Be careful not to whack your buddies in the head with your ankle as you come around.

▶ Once he has completed the turn, Blue pulls his right leg in tight to White's side and sits on White's chest.

If your opponent tries to defend by bracing with his arms to keep you from spinning, turn the opposite way, step over, and you have the mount.

▶ Blue drops his left knee to the floor and establishes the top mount.

Blue is standing in White's Open Guard. White puts his feet on Blue's hips. Blue reaches under White's left ankle with his left hand and grabs the cloth below the knee. Blue also grabs White's right sleeve with his left hand.

Blue steps back with his left foot.

Blue steps back with his right foot, making space between his hips and White's feet. As Blue steps back with his right foot, he simultaneously pulls White's feet toward his right as he pulls White's right arm toward his left, causing White's body to rotate counter clockwise.

Now that he has cleared White's feet, Blue forward and goes to the knee on belly position. Notice Blue maintains his grips and pulls White's right arm straight up.

Blue steps over White's head with his left foot and lowers his hips, sitting close to White's shoulder as he grabs White's wrist with his right hand.

Blue falls back for the armbar. He uses his leg against White's face to prevent White from sitting up as he sits back.

White has Blue in the Open Guard, his feet on Blue's hips. Blue holds the cloth inside White's knees.

Blue moves his hips to his left and pushes White's legs to the right side, making White believe he is going to pass around to the right.

When White resists by pulling his legs to his right, Blue suddenly reverses the force and pushes both of White's legs down to his (White's) right, and simultaneously moves around White's left side.

Blue leans all his weight into White and pushes White's legs down to the mat at White's right side.

Blue lowers his body, gets control of the hezd and establishes side control.

Blue is standing in White's Open Guard, holding the cloth inside White's knees, thumbs in.

Blue lowers his level, circling his right elbow under White's left knee (maintain the grip on the inside of the knee).

Blue pushes off with his right foot, twisting his body to his left and pushing White's left knee across his body, and passes around White's left side.

Here is a different view of the grips and position of the elbow.

❂ Use the power of your legs and body to push the opponent's leg across, not just the upper body.

The finish of the Guard pass is a matter of forward pressure. Be wary of an opponent's attemps to go to his knees.
More on preventing that next.

Here, as Blue attempts to pass the Guard with double underhooks, there is a lot of space. If Blue does nothing to prevent it, White is likely to attempt going to his knees by spinning away from Blue.

Blue pulls in with the grip across White's throat as he drives his right knee forward and over White's arm. Blue drops to his knees close to White's side.

Holding himself down close to White, Blue reaches up with his left hand and pulls White's legs off his head for the pass.

A common defense to stacking type attacks is for the bottom player to roll back over a shoulder into the turtle position. Here are two ways to prevent a player from going to his knees by using your legs.

In this situation, as Blue attempts to pass White's Guard with the double underhooks, Blue steps on White's biceps with his foot to pin down White's upper body, and to prevent White from turning to the turtle position.

Grabbing the cloth at White's knees, Blue bends forward and pulls White's legs off his head.

Sometimes a player focuses so much of his effort on preventing you from coming around or under his legs that he does not defend against your coming over the top. This technique works well against opponents with shorter legs. Elements of boldness and surprise are key.

◀▶ Blue is standing in White's Open Guard. White has his feet hooked inside Blue's knees. Blue holds the insides of White's knees, and uses his weight to push White's right leg to the mat.

◀▶ Blue moves his right elbow up and begins to push back on White's left leg. He wants to drive White's foot to the mat.

◀▶ Blue shoves White's left leg between his legs and turns his hips as he begins to lower his weight.

⊙ This one often results in a half-guard situation. Passing the half-guard is examined in the next chapter.

◀▶ Blue drops his weight and his left knee over White's right leg to top mount.

White sits up in Open Guard.

Blue grabs behind White's collar with his left hand.

Blue leans forward and posts his right hand on the mat in between White's feet.

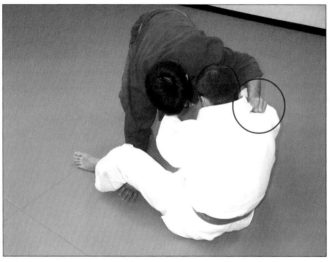

Note the placement of Blue's hand on White's back. When he jumps, most of Blue's weight will be on the flooor. He will use the hand on White's back mostly for control and balance.

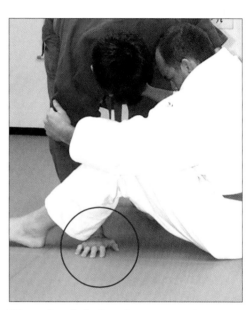

Here the right hand posts on the mat.

Blue pushes off with both feet and springs over White in a cartwheel motion, twisting his body in the air.

Blue lands on both feet behind White, and grabs White's chest lapel with his right hand.

Blue falls back to the mat, pulling White back with him as he puts his hooks in to take the back.

Note: *it is not necessary to get vertical, as in this picture, to pull off the move.*

This pass can also be done with the right hand posted on the opponent's knee instead of the mat. Obviously, however, the knee is not going to be as stable.

◀▶ White has Blue in his Open Guard. Blue holds inside White's knees.

◀▶ Blue moves back and forces White's feet to the mat with his weight.

❷ Make sure to put some of your weight onto the outside of your shin and your opponent's side. Doing so helps immobilize his torso.

❷ This is a timing move, be quick.

◀▶ Blue steps his right foot between White's legs and across toward White's right hip.

◀▶ As his right foot touches the mat, Blue shifts his weight forward, so that his right knee is pressing down on White's hips and he begins to step up with his left foot. As he steps through, Blue releases his left grip and grabs White's right sleeve.

◀▶ Blue steps his left foot forward and out to the side as he passes the Guard and establishes the knee in belly position.

◀▶ In the Open Guard, Blue pushes White's legs up and pushes his pelvis forward, moving up to sit over the backs of White's legs.

◀▶ Blue sits all his weight on top of White, and by bringing his knees slightly together, pinches White's legs into one another. This helps to control White's hips momentarily.

◀▶ Blue swings his right foot across White's hips and all the way across his body until Blue's foot is outside White's right hip.

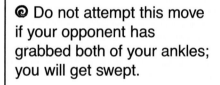

☻ Do not attempt this move if your opponent has grabbed both of your ankles; you will get swept.

◀▶ Blue turns his hips and uses his weight to press White's legs to the mat. Blue simultaneously lays his body on top of White's torso. Blue maintains constant pressure on top of his opponent as he does the move. The contact point of the pressure begins with the inside of the upper thigh, then to his butt, then to his hip.

◀▶ Just before Blue's right foot touches the mat, he twists his body back to the right, swinging his left foot over White's legs and lands on his knees in side control.

A video sequence of this pass appears at page 86.

White controls Blue with the Spider Guard, holding the sleeve with the foot on the biceps.

Blue lowers his body and ducks his head under White's left leg, pushing up with the back of his head behind White's knee.

Blue leans his weight into White and looks upward as he steps through with his left foot. The step and upward pressure push White's left foot up off Blue's right biceps, freeing Blue's arm.

Blue pivots on his left foot and swings his right foot around to face White from the side.

▲This column illustrates Blue's body movement during the pass.

◉ Blue makes a wide base.

◉ Keeping his back straight, Blue lowers his head.

◉ Blue steps through with his left foot, lifts his head and looks upward as he thrusts his hips forward.

◉ Make sure as you step through that you keep pressure on the opponent's leg with the back of your neck.

Blue establishes side control.

In this variation, White controls Blue's left sleeve, so Blue cannot reach across with his left hand to grab White's leg (see next page).

Blue lowers his body and ducks his head under White's left leg.

Driving forward off his toes, Blue looks upward and begins to *shuffle* around to his right. The difference from the last technique is that Blue does not turn his hips for this one.

Blue underhooks White's head and comes to side control.

(CONTINUED FROM PG. 83)

No one wins all the time, not even Tori.

White executes the *Over and Back* pass.

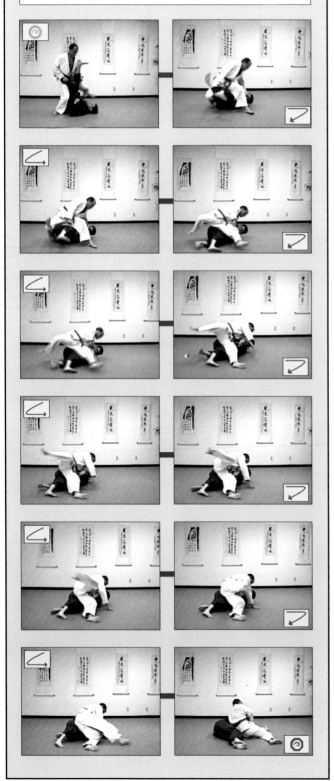

This is a variation of the pass from the preceding page. Blue is in White's Spider Guard.

In this Variation, Blue reaches across with his left hand and grabs over the top of White's left thigh.

Blue and looks upward as he pulls White's left leg to his left with his left hand. Blue simultaneously steps his left leg across to his right ducks his head under White's leg.

Blue pivots around his left foot and swings his right leg around.

Blue establishes side control

This is another variation of the duckunder pass. Blue is in White's Spider Guard.

Blue reaches across with his left hand and grabs over the top of White's left thigh.

Blue lowers his head and ducks under White's left leg.

In this variation, Blue does not step across with his left leg, he sprawls and maintaining forward pressure into White, shuffles his feet around to his right As he pulls White's left leg toward his left.

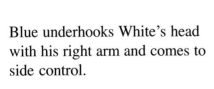

Blue underhooks White's head with his right arm and comes to side control.

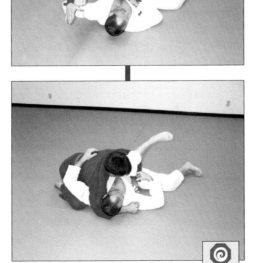

Blue stands in White's Open Guard. Blue holds the cloth inside White's knees.

Blue hops back, bends forward and pushes White's feet to the mat with his body weight.

Blue pushes White's knees down and leapfrogs over White's knees. Blue continues to push White's knees until he clears them.

Blue thrusts his hips forward and drops to his knees and top mount.

As Blue attempts the *leapfrog pass*, White defends by pushing up behind Blue's legs in an attempt to throw Blue over his head.

Blue counters by leaning to one side and scissoring his legs. The momentum carries him through a 3/4 turn and into side control.

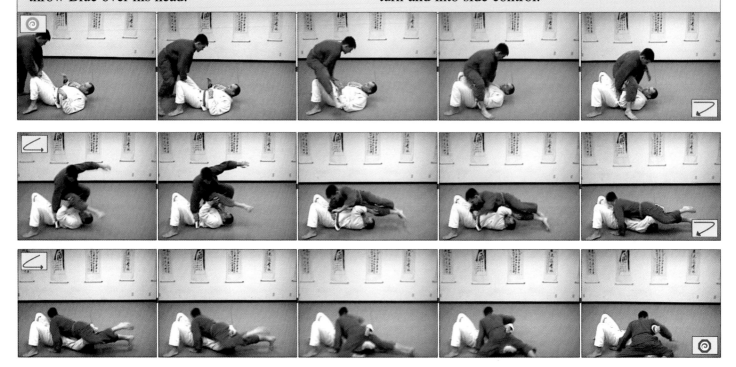

Blue is standing in White's Open Guard, with grips inside White's knees (thumbs down).

Blue leans forward with his weight to pin White's feet to the mat, and lowers his head between White's legs, posting the top of his head on the mat.

Blue pushes off with both feet and lifts both feet into the air.

Blue bridges over White and his feet land on White's left side. Blue is still holding White's legs.

Blue now releases his grips and quickly twists so tha he is chest to chest with White.

Blue stands in White's Open Guard and holds inside White's knees.

Blue twists his hips to the right, and moves his right leg outside White's left foot.

Blue leans his weight into the outside of White's leg as he spins. He will keep contact and pressure on White throughout the turn.

As he completes the spin, Blue lets go with his right hand and drops his hips onto White.

Blue continues turning, bringing his right leg over to establish side control.

◉ Blue must momentarily remove the soles of White's feet from his hips. He does so with a combination of footwork, a twist of the hips, and a quick pop with his arms. Blue lets his weight crash down as he turns.

There must be constant weight on, and contact with, the opponent's leg/body throughout the spin. This is to limit the opponent's mobility. It serves the added benefit of giving you feedback as to where he is for the instant that your back is turned.

Here is an interesting one. Instead of passing the guard, White goes straight for Blue's back.

Blue stacks White on his shoulders, pushing White's feet over his head.

Blue pushes his left palm down on the back of White's left knee to hold him down. At the same time, Blue steps his right foot across to the side of White's right hip.

Blue swings his left foot over White's legs, and sits on the back of White's legs.

Blue hooks his right foot over the top of White's right hip, and turns to his left, laying down onto his left side. As he turns, Blue grabs the back of White's belt with both hands.

Blue pulls White into him, then grabs over the top of White's shoulder. Blue pulls White's upper body into him and sets his hooks in.

Blue reaches around White's neck with his free hand, and completes taking White's back.

❷ To prevent being passed a player will fend with their legs from whatever position necessary. These two techniques address a North/South situation.

White has spun under to prevent the pass. White has lifted his feet over his head and pushes Blue off with both feet on Blue's chest.

Blue lowers his head and grabs underneath White's armpits with both hands.

Blue sprawls his feet back and drives his head into White's gut as he pulls up and in with his hands. Blue pushes out with his elbows to make space.

Blue continues driving his head forward and pulling in until he flattens Blue and establishes control.

In this variation, White has attempted the same defense, bringing his feet back over his head and

pushing Blue's chest away. Blue grabs with both hands, four fingers in at the sides of White's collar.

Using the power of his legs and hips, Blue begins to stand and pull up with his hands.

As Blue pulls White's upper body up off the mat, White's lower body cannot help but drop.

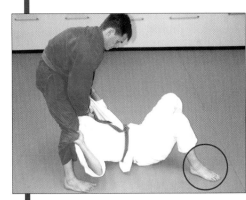

The instant White's feet hit the floor, Blue quickly drops on top of him and establishes control.

CHAPTER 4

While attempting to pass your opponent's Guard, you must always be on guard against attacks. Your opponent should be continuously attempting to submit or sweep you. The most important element of the Guard pass is to maintain your balance at all times. Because of the dynamic nature of the Guard fight, you will need to make constant adjustments in position, grips and center of gravity. It is also important to understand which offensive techniques are available to your opponent from various positions and grips. The best time to stop an attack is as early as possible. Remaining aware of your opponent's position, movement and grips will allow you to adjust your own position to your advantage before you are caught in a threatening situation. The best way to develop the sensitivity necessary to maintain your base while passing the Guard is through sparring drills. In most BJJ academies, a great deal amount of time is spent on practicing the techniques of attacking from and passing the Guard.

Once you are caught in a disadvantageous position, or the opponent has caught you in a submission technique, you will need to apply a defensive technique, and possibly a counter-offensive of your own. Although stopping your opponent's attack as early as possible is best, sometimes you will find yourself 'caught' in a submission attempt. There are specific guidelines and techniques designed to handle these types of situations. It is important to practice these escapes and counters from disadvantageous positions on a regular basis. Once you have successfully defended your opponent's attack, you ideally will continue with a counter-offensive technique. You may move from a defensive technique into a Guard pass, or into a submission technique of your own (most often leg attacks). It is bears repeating that maintaining a solid base and adjusting to keep your balance as necessary is the best way to avoid being caught by the opponent's attack.

White sits up and wraps his right arm around Blue's neck.

White grabs his right wrist with his left hand and falls back to lock his Guard to finish the choke. As White falls back, Blue wraps his right arm around White's neck.

Blue pulls down on White's shoulder and pushes the other way with his head.

Blue sprawls onto the balls of his feet and walks forward as far as he can, squeezing White's neck and pressing his right shoulder into White's throat. White will not have enough leverage to finish the choke (It is very important to continue driving forward and press the weight into the opponent's throat).

Blue walks his feet up as far as possible and smashes his weight into White's throat to defend the choke. Blue can also use his free arm to take off White's arm.

White puts his right hand inside Blue's right lapel to set up a cross choke. Blue immediately holds down White's free arm with his right hand, to prevent the completion of the choke.

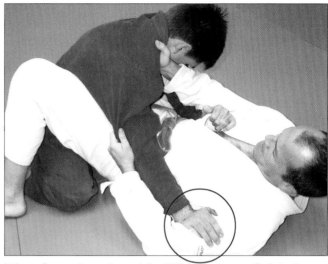

View from the other side. White cannot finish the choke with one arm. Blue needs to be wary of White switching to an attack of his right arm.

White sets up for a cross choke. Blue pulls down on White's left arm with his right hand, first to prevent White from getting the grip he wants. And then to prevent him from drawing his elbow outwards.

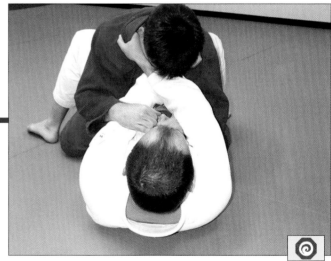

Blue tucks his chin down against his chest to protect his neck.

As White sets his first grip, Blue slides his right hand up inside White's wrist. This takes pressure off the carotid artery thus killing the choke. Here, Blue also pushes White's right elbow away and across his body. This relieves pressure also.

Some opponents generate enough power to fininsh chokes even if you have put your own hand in for defense; they can chokc you with pressure through your own hand. Pushing the elbow helps prevent this.

This is a cross choke defense if the opponent already has the cross grip position. White sets the choke. Blue pulls down on White's lower (left) elbow with his right hand and pushes White's top (right) elbow away with his left hand to make space between white's arms.

Blue continues to pull down with his right arm and push away with his left. Blue has killed the choke at this point. If White won't let go Blue can pass his head through the space between White's arms, or protect with his hand as in the next frame.

Blue threads his right arm between White's arms and reaches his right palm up beside the right side of his head to protect his neck.

White puts his right hand inside Blue's right lapel to set up a cross choke. Blue immediately holds down White's free arm with his right hand, to prevent the completion of the choke.

Blue slides his left hand up under White's right armpit. Blue levers up a little off of his own wrist to raise White's elbow to allow space for Blue to duck his head under.

Blue ducks his head and circles it to his right underneath White's wrist to remove the threat of the cross choke.

Blue has now "uncrossed" White's grip, extricating himself in the process.

ATTACK

Blue grabs inside White's right lapel with his right hand, four fingers in.

Blue brings his left leg over to the left side of White's neck. Blue pulls with his right hand and pushes with his left leg, choking White.

DEFENSE

White attempts to choke Blue as described above. Blue grabs his right lapel with his right hand.

Blue jerks his lapel out of White's grip, releasing the choke.

Before an opponent can take your arm he must establish a position to do so. You can prevent armbars - or any other type of submission - by preventing your opponent from putting together the elements necessary for his attack. For instance, before the armbar can be successfully applied the attacker will need to move his hips in the direction of the arm he is attacking. If the player on top adusts his base immediately so that he remains centered with the attacker, the attack will fail.

◀ Blue shows a correct method of holding the opponent for an **armbar from the Guard:**

- ❂ Blue's hips are high under White's right armpit.
- ❂ The fulcrum of Blue's leverage is above White's elbow joint.
- ❂ Blue pinches his knees together.
- ❂ Blue keeps pressure on White's head with the back of his left leg.
- ❂ Blue's body is at approximately a 90 degree angle to White's.
- ❂ Blue holds White's wrist with both hands (there are a variety of ways to hold the arm).
- ❂ White's thumb points away from Blue's chest.
- ❂ Blue raises his hips to finish the move.

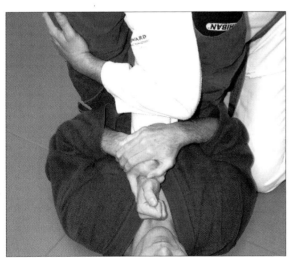

◀ Close up of the hand position:

- ❂ Blue holds the wrist at the juncture of the wrist and palm, making it difficult for White to rotate his arm away from the pressure.
- ❂ Blue also keeps his elbows locked tight to his sides for more power.

Here is an example of the principal discussed above. As White pulls Blue's right arm in to set up an armbar, Blue moves his left arm inside White's leg in anticipation of the coming attack.

As White pulls Blue's right arm across his chest, Blue braces it against being pulled across his body with his other arm. Even if White gets Blue's right arm where he wants it, the position of Blue's elbow next to White's left thigh prevents White from squeezing his knees together and performing the attack.

White controls Blue's right arm and brings his right leg high, pushing inward to break Blues' posture.

As White attempts to bring his left leg over Blue's head, Blue catches behind White's lower leg with his left hand.

Blue pulls White's left leg down and across.

Blue smashes his weight onto White's legs to control his hips, and frees his arm.

With his arms free and both of Whites legs to one side, Blue has all but passed White's Guard.

White sets up the armbar. Blue is ready and immediately begins his defense. He starts by opening his hand.

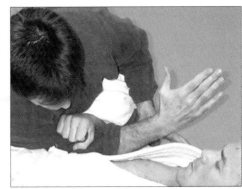

White begins to pass his leg over Blue's head. Blue puts his right palm on his left biceps, and bends his left arm to prevent his right arm from straightening.

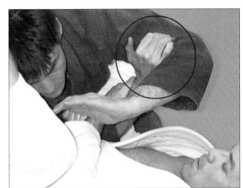

As White passes his left leg over Blue's head, Blue pushes down with his left palm on the back of White's leg. As Blue pushes down on White's leg, he also lowers his upper body down, using his weight to smash White's leg down.

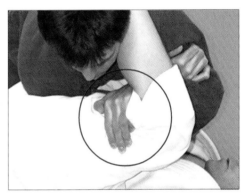

Blue smashes all his weight onto White's legs, pushing his knees into his face and raising White's hips off the ground.

Blue keeps his weight down and maintains the downward pressure behind White's left leg as he jerks his right arm free. Pull the elbow out in sudden and forceful spurts, inching it out if need be.

1. This variation is used when the opponent has the armbar almost completely set up. White catches Blue's right arm in an armbar.

2. Blue hooks his right hand inside his left elbow crook to keep White from straightening the elbow.

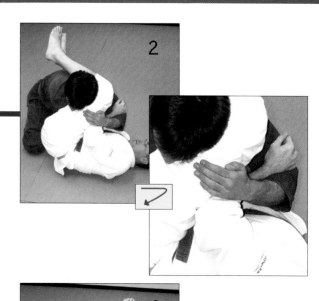

3. Blue drives forward and stacks White up onto his shoulders, lifting White's hips off the ground. Blue simultaneously lays his upper body weight onto the back of White's legs to preventing him from straightening his legs and hips. Blue puts his left knee beside White's head and puts his right knee up behind White's hips, preventing him from moving his hips.

4. Keeping his weight down, Blue works his left hand up between White's legs and hooks his palm over the back of White's left thigh.

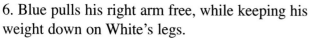

5. Blue keeps his weight pressing down on White and his palm pushing down on the back of White's left leg as he pulls his right elbow out.

6. Blue pulls his right arm free, while keeping his weight down on White's legs.

7. Blue reaches his right hand across and grabs thumb inside of White's right collar.

8. Blue moves around to his right while he presses down on White's throat, passing the Guard.

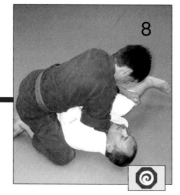

White catches Blue's right arm in an armbar.

Blue grabs behind White's neck with his left hand.

Blue smashes his weight down onto White, pulling himself down with is left hand, forcing White's knees into his face. At the same time, Blue slides his left knee near White's head and puts his right knee up behind White's hips.

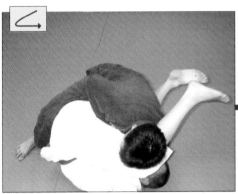

Keeping his weight down, Blue begins to pull his right elbow backward.

Blue frees his right arm.

Blue pushes White's legs across to his left with his right hand (pushing outside White's left knee).

Blue moves around to his right and passes White's Guard.

White catches Blue's right arm in an armbar.

Blue brings his weight forward and smashes White to prevent White from extending his hips.

White counters by extending and rolling face down for an armbar.

Blue jumps over White's body.

Blue lands on White's left side.

Blue immediately grabs the back of White's neck with his left hand, and grabs around the inside of White's left leg with his right arm.

Here is another veiw of the spinning part of the escape.

White pivots underneath Blue and continues the pressure with a face down armbar. Blue twists his right arm thumb up to relieve the pressure on his elbow.

Blue quickly shuffles his feet to his right.

Blue spreads his base and drives forward into side control.

Blue twists his right thumb upward to relieve the pressure on his elbow.

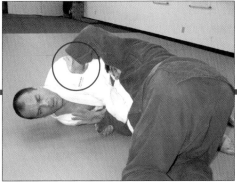

Blue follows through by coming around 270 degrees. Note how he pushes with his free hand to help him come around.

Blue follows through by pushing White onto his back and taking control of White's head.

ATTACK

  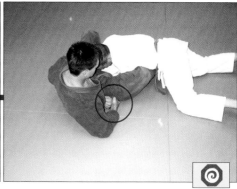

White attempts to pass Blue's Guard with double underhooks. Blue scoots his hips back and grabs White's left wrist with his right hand.

Blue inserts his right foot all the way across White's hips. The grip on White's wrist is key. Blue pins it to his hip and pulls up on it.

Blue hooks his right foot on the outside of White's right hip. Blue straightens his right leg for a shoulder lock submission.

Opposite view.

DEFENSE

Blue counters the above technique by grabbing White's right ankle and preventing him from hooking it on his right hip.

White catches Blue's left arm in a coiled shoulder lock (omo plata) with the legs.

Blue does a forward shoulder roll to escape the lock.

As Blue lands, he controls White's legs and comes up into his base.

⊙ Blue always rolls over the shoulder of the arm which is trapped, when using this escape.

White sets up the shoulder lock. Blue grabs his belt to defend.

Blue lifts his left leg up and begins to slide it over the top of White's chest.

Blue slides his leg over White and drops his left knee on White's left side.

Blue sits up in his base and uses his legs and back to straighten up and pull his left arm free.

White attacks with the omo platta. Blue grabs his belt to stop White from finishing him quickly.

Because White is controlling Blue's hips with his right arm, Blue is unable to roll forward to escape.

Blue begins to slide onto his right hip.

White catches Blue with the omo plata.

Blue grabs his belt to defend the leverage.

❷ Blue posts on his foot and hand to facillitate swinging his body underneath White. The action is like a pendulum. It is important that Blue generate a bit of momentum. Blue must also pull White across as he goes under.

Blue rolls to his left, pulling White over his body. Note how he grabs the pants to move White's leg.

White lands on Blue's left side. Blue changes his grip to help pull himself up.

Blue comes up and rolls White into side control.

Blue begins to twist onto his right side, sliding his right knee underneath White's right hip.

Blue continues to twist to his left as he pulls White on top of his hips.

Blue moves underneath White and pulls him over his body to his left side. Blue will then come up behind White on White's left side.

White catches Blue with the omo plata. Blue grabs his own pants to defend the leverage.

Blue posts his right leg and hand out to the side for base

◎ This technique requires some strength. It is not very effective against larger opponents. This is not to say that it does not have its place.

Note the solid base established by Blue before he tries to lift.

The very first thing is to protect the arm. By grabbing his own clothes, Blue inhibits White's opportunity to finish.

Be extra careful practicing and performing this one. It is dangerous to the neck of the guy on the bottom, especially if his head comes off the ground and then drops back down.

Blue lifts up his upper body and grabs his left wrist with his right.

Blue uses the power of his legs and back to straighten up and lift White up off the mat.

The force causes White to flip over backward onto his knees, allowing Blue to free his arm and move to control White from the top.

Note that Blue looks to the ceiling. This helps generare power to lift White.

The time to apply this one is while White is on his back. Once he sits up, forget about it.

ATTACK

▶ White is in Blue's Open Guard. Blue controls White's right sleeve and hooks his right ankle over White's right hip.

▶ Blue wraps his left leg over the top of White's right arm, inserting his left ankle into White's elbow crook.

▶ As White begins to pass around to Blue's right side, Blue triangles his legs, his left ankle hooked behind his right knee. Blue pulls tight on White's arm.

▶ As White passes around the right side of Blue's Guard, Blue reaches up with both hands around White's upper arm and pulls down with both hands as he drops his left knee toward the mat for a keylock on White's right arm.

▶ Close up of the leg position from the other side.

DEFENSE

▶ White catches Blue's arm in a keylock.

▶ Blue moves back into White's Guard, posts his right foot for base and grabs around White's left leg with his left arm, pulling Whie's leg up so that White cannot apply pressure downward with his leg.

▶ Blue pulls White's left knee up and in.

▶ Blue pulls his right arm free.

▶ Blue is now safe to pass the Guard.

DEFENSE

▶ White catches Blue's right arm in a keylock.

▶ Blue grabs around the back of White's neck with his left hand and lifts White up onto his shoulders.

▶ Blue smashes White laying his weight onto White's chest.

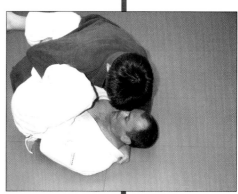

▶ With his thumb in the back of White's collar, Blue circles his left elbow around White's head.

▶ Blue holds White's hips off the mat and crushes his throat with his left forearm.

Elements of the triangle choke:

☯ Blue has his right shin across the back of White's neck, parallel with an imaginary line across the top of White's shoulders.
☯ Blue locks his right ankle behind his left knee.
☯ Blue pulls White's right arm across his body and pulls down on White's head.
☯ He squeezes his knees together and lifts his hips.
☯ Pressure from White's own shoulder into his neck aids the choke.

> ◉ Remember, the best defense is to prevent the submission attempt from ever becoming a serious threat. This is a good first option against the triangle.

White begins to set up a triangle choke. Blue reacts by anchoring his right hand and assuming a solid, upright posture.

Blue immediately grabs inside of White's right leg and pulls outward. At the same time, Blue straightens his back and lifts his head up as high as possible.

Blue pushes upward with his hips, lifting his rear up off his heels and breaks the hold.
◉ Keep your posture and follow up right away. Beware of armbars.

White sets up the triangle choke. Blue pulls White's right leg outward with his left hand while lifting his head as high as possible.

Blue reaches around White's right leg with his left and grabs with thumb inside White's collar.

Blue smashes forward with all his weight and moves around to his left side while putting pressure across White's throat.

Continuing to smash down and move around to his right, the pressure behind White's right leg causes his legs to open.

Blue passes the Guard.

Blue gets caught in a triangle choke that is locked on tight. Blue pulls outward on White's right leg to relieve some of the pressure.

Blue thrusts his body forward and towards his left, putting pressure inside White's right leg. The move should be sudden and forceful.

Blue continues to drive his chest forward and pulls outward on White's right leg to open White's feet.

Blue is caught in a tight triangle. He grabs White's right leg and pulls outward with his left hand.

Blue turns his body to his left, and begins to push into White's legs.

Blue pushes off his feet and drives his weight into White's legs at a perpendicular angle (Blue's and White's torsos are 90 degrees to each other). The pressure unlocks White's feet.

Blue drives forward and passes the Guard.

White locks the triangle choke on Blue.

Blue pulls out on White's right leg with his left hand and begins to stand.

Blue puts his right knee directly in the center of White's rear.

Blue steps his left foot behind his right, and squats down which causes his right knee to wedge up between White's legs.

❷ The idea here is to use your body weight and leverage to wedge in a kneecap. As Blue sits back, most of his weight is on his right leg. The left leg is used for stability. Bringing in the kneecap has the effect of opening the opponent's legs and relieving pressure on the neck.

As Blue drives his right knee up and lifts his head, the pressure of his right leg wedging between White's legs causes White's legs to open.

White catches Blue in a triangle choke.

Blue hugs White's right leg with his right to protect his arm and grabs White's right sleeve with his left hand as he stands.

Blue steps his left foot on top of White's right arm.

Blue's leg pushes off White's arm into the mat as he lays down and back to his side. At the same time he pulls White's leg off of his head.

Blue sits on his hip and pulls his head out of the choke.

Blue frees his head. He must immediately be ready if White attempts to switch to an attack against the arm still between White's legs.

Blue is caught in a triangle choke.

Blue stands, moves to his left and hooks his hand over the side of White's neck.

Blue steps over White's head.

Blue sits back and straightens his body. Blue uses his leg to put pressure on White's neck as he does so.

Blue hugs White's right leg tightly to prevent the armbar as he pushes White's head away with his leg and arches his body back to break the triangle.

◉ Blue must be wary of a follow up armbar attempt.

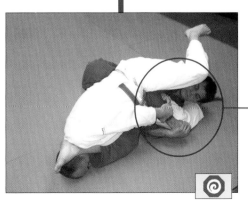

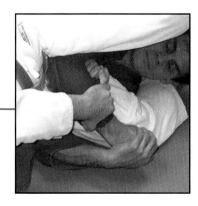

FROM THE HALF GUARD

White sits up and grabs Blue's left wrist with his right hand, he intends to attempt a Kimura

White reaches over Blue's left arm with his left arm and grabs his own right wrist, trapping Blue's arm.

As White lays back to the mat and attempts to pull Blue's left arm behind his back for a shoulder lock, Blue immediately grabs his own belt to protect his arm.

FROM THE GUARD

In this sequence Blue attempts a similar defense.

Instead of reaching through and grabbing his trapped arm with his free one, Blue grabs his own gi.

Blue leans his weight onto White, smashing White's right upper arm to the mat and restricting White's motion and power.

Continuing the downward pressure, Blue presses his weight forward and begins to pull his right hand through to the front of his hips. Blue grabs his own left wrist with his right hand and pulls his arm through.

If White does not pull his arm free he will be submitted with a shoulder crank.

Blue continues pulling his left wrist up and through with his right hand, causing White's left arm to bend backward until he abandons his grip or submits.

Blue uses his free hand for base and begins to straighten himself up.

Blue switches the free hand to White's hip. He is pushing his torso both forward and up. A good deal of the pressure on White is transmitted through the top of Blue's right shoulder.

If White does not let go he will get submitted.

This variation is not as effective as the half guard version. The leverage is not as good.

Here is a common sweep from the guard. Part of any defense is understanding the attack.

▶ Blue holds White in his Closed Guard. Blue pulls down on White's collar and waits for him to resist backward.

▶ As White pulls back, Blue follows the motion and begins to sit up, posting on his left elbow, opening his feet as he pulls his right foot back and reaches over the top of White's right shoulder with his right arm.

▶ Continuing the momentum, Blue raises his hips and posts on his left palm and right foot. He begins to twist to his left.

▶ Blue's hips knock White's torso. The movement is forward and in a circle to Blue's left.

▶ Blue lands in the mount.

▶ As White begins to sit up and sweep, Blue immediately leans forward and pushes White back down with his right hand.

▶ White is pushed back onto the mat. It is important to push the opponent down with the hand on the side to which the opponent attempts to sweep (ex: if the opponent attempts to sweep you to your right side, push him down with your right hand).

▶ White has already sat up and reached over Blue's shoulder. Blue leans forward and locks his arms around White's body.

▶ Blue drives off his knees and twists to his left.

▶ Blue drives White down to the mat.

▶ In this variation, White is even further into the sweep. Blue drives forward, hugs White's body with his right arm and pushes down on White's right inside knee.

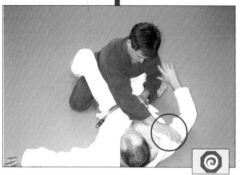

▶ Blue continues to drive his weight forward.

▶ Blue pushes White's right leg down and begins to bring his left knee up and over White's right leg.

▶ Blue continues to push forward, driving his left knee to the mat over White's right leg.

If Blue gets his knee over he will be in a good position to pass.

ATTACK

White stands up in Blue's Guard.

Blue hooks around the inside of White's right leg with his left arm as he posts his right hand over his head.

Blue moves his left hip inside White's right knee.

DEFENSE

Blue stands in White's Guard. White's sets up the takedown as described above.

Blue twists his hips to the left and drives his right knee into White's chest. This prevents White from bridging into Blue's right leg.

Blue continues to twist his hips and drive his knee down. The pressure breaks White's Guard open.

Blue pushes off with his right hands and begins to push his hips into White's inside right knee.

The pressure causes Blue to fall onto his back.

Blue continues up to the mount position.

Blue drops his weight onto White.

Blue reaches his right arm around White's left leg and drives his hips downward, clearing White's feet.

Blue moves into side control.

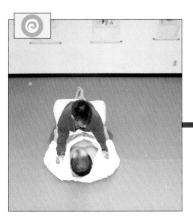

Blue is in White's Guard.

Blue stands.

As Blue stands up to break the Guard, White reaches forward for Blue's ankles.

White grabs behind Blue's ankles and opens his Guard.

White extends his legs and pushes Blue backwards. As Blue falls, he turns onto his left side and swings his right leg over the top of White's right leg, putting his right foot on the front of White's right hip.

Blue wraps White's left ankle with his right arm.

Blue grabs his right wrist with his left hand and pulls up as he arches back for the straight ankle lock.

Close up of Blue's grip. Be sure to pinch your knees tightly when applying the ankle lock.

● De La Riva style attacks require sleeve grips and/or a grip on the back.
● Prevent the grips to stop the attacks. Here White has good grips.
● There are many opportunities to attack White's leg for Blue. Here Blue is using his arms as base and to keep White from sitting up and transitioning into a leg attack.

White has inserted his right leg through Blue's legs. Blue pushes White's left knee down to the mat by lowering his weight.

Blue grabs White's right ankle with his right hand.

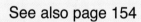

See also page 154

Blue steps his right foot back and pushes White's right ankle down, clearing his right leg.

Blue immediately steps his right leg over the top of White's left leg and drives his left knee over the top of White's hip to pass.

ATTACK

Blue prepares to attack with a sweep from the **Butterfly Guard**:
❷ Blue has both feet hooked inside White's legs.
❷ Blue has one arm (or both) under White's arm(s), holding his belt at the rear.
❷ Blue's other hand is holding over White's arm.
❷ Blue is off-center of White, his weight sits mostly to one side (his right).

DEFENSE

White sits up into the Butterfly Guard and grips Blue.   White underhooks with his left arm.

Blue pummels his right arm inside and underneath White's left arm.

Blue holds around White's back in an underarm bear hug position.

White puts both hooks inside Blue's legs, sits up, and locks his arms around Blue's body in an underarm bear hug. This is a bad position for Blue.

Blue is at risk of being swept, and so must move to a more stable position. As White leans back to sweep, Blue follows and puts his palms under White's chin.

Blue arches his back and pushes White's chin, causing White's head to turn to his right.

Blue continues to push White's chin away as he moves his hips back, breaking the waist lock.

White sits up to the Butterfly Guard position. Blue grabs behind White's neck with his left hand.

Blue stops White from attacking by raising his body and using his weight to push down on the back of White's neck. This causes White's head to go down so that he cannot bring his power forward.

White sits up and hooks his right leg around the outside of Blues' left leg, preparing for a sweep or single leg takedown.

Blue pushes down on the back of White's head to stop his attacking forward pressure.

CHAPTER 5

PASSING THE HALF GUARD

Half Guard is when you have one leg free and one leg caught between your opponent's legs. The position frequently occurs as you attempt to pass the Guard; your opponent will attempt to catch you in the Half Guard to prevent the full pass. You may also opt to go into your opponent's Half Guard voluntarily, as the first step in passing a difficult Guard. It is important to be aware of the options you have when caught in the Half Guard, and also to be aware of the options of your opponent.

When you are in the top position in the Half Guard, your opponent's first options are usually to either try to sweep you to the bottom position or put you back in the Guard. The sweep will cost you points. Being put back in the Guard means you are in greater danger of attack, and will have to start your pass all over again. If the fighter on the bottom manages to move around to your back while you are on all fours, it counts the same as a sweep. The opponent also has the option of attempting to apply a knee bar from the bottom.

Obviously, being put back in the Guard is preferable to being swept . You will receive a vantage point for gaining the Half Guard position, so going into the opponent's Half Guard and then being put back in the Guard results in an advantage for you.

To prevent the sweep or reversal, control your opponent's head and to keep your hips as low (there are, of course, exceptions). Just like passing the full Guard, passing the Half Guard sometimes requires patience and a methodical approach.

In order to pass the Half Guard and gain side control or the full mount, you must free your trapped leg. There are a number of techniques and variations to free the leg and pass. Most involve maintaining control of the opponent's head/shoulder area and keeping your hips as low. It is also important for many of the passes to prevent your opponent from controlling your outside (free leg side) knee or hip. Underhooking the opponent's arm or keeping your hip pressed tightly to the mat will help prevent the opponent from lifting your outside leg or hip. You can also use your free leg to push down on the opponent's legs as you pull your trapped leg free.

There are also a number of submissions that can be set up and completed from the top position in Half Guard. When on top of your opponent in the Half Guard, you can attack his far arm with an American Lock. You can also choke your opponent with a sleeve choke, and attack with variations of the shoulder lock.

Once you pass the Half Guard, you should end up in the side control or the mount, good positions from which to attack.

Know your options in the Half Guard and the options of your opponent.

White catches Blue in the Half Guard.

Holding under White's left arm with his right, Blue reaches his left arm over White's head.

Blue toes his foot in again, moving closer to White's rear which causes his right knee to push upward. His objective at this point is to get his knee tot the other side of White's leg.

Once he gets his knee through, the rest of his leg comes through easily unless White triangles his foot. *(Getting a trinagled foot free is covered ahead.)*

The same technique as above.

Blue grips White's belt at the rear with his left hand (White' head is behind Blue's left armpit). At the same time, Blue begins to push down on the inside of White's left knee.

Blue pushes down on White's knee while walking his right foot upward, toward White's rear. Here Blue toes in his foot, pivoting on the heel.

Continuing to push down on White' knee, Blue pivots on the ball of his foot, moving his heel closer to White's rear.

Blue pulls his right knee through White's legs.

Blue reaches underneath White's left arm, twists his hips to the right and lowers his right knee to the mat.

Close up of the grips in the mount.

Note how Blue locks his arm out. It takes much less strength to hold things away with the arm straight.

White holds Blue in the Half Guard. Blue underhooks White's neck with his left arm and with the other hand grabs White's left lapel just above the belt.

Blue pulls the bottom of White's gi out of his belt and feeds it below White's left armpit. This grip prevents White from bridging and mounting Blue as he escapes.

Blue feeds the cloth to his left hand with his right hand and grips tightly.

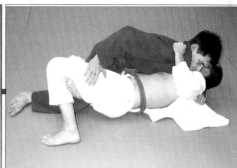

Here is the technique from a different angle.

Note that even when Blue lifts his hips he keeps them relatively low.

Blue lifts his hips a little and slides his left shin across the top of White's hips.

Blue lowers his left hip to the mat.

Blue pushes forward with his left shin on top of White' thighs and pulls his right foot free. Blue is now able to establish side control.

◉ Sometimes a little bit more is needed to get your foot free. Blue gets the extra mechanical advantage he needs by putting his left foot on top of White's right thigh to lever open White's thighs.

Blue has his right leg caught in White' Half Guard. Blue underhooks White's neck with his left arm and pushes outward on the inside of White's left knee. Blue pulls his right knee up until it clears White' legs.

Keeping his hips as low as possible, Blue twists his hips to his left, simultaneously underhooking White's neck with his right arm.

Hugging White's neck tightly, Blue continues twisting his hips to the left, driving his right knee across the top of White's hips. Blue puts his right knee down outside White's right hip.

Blue posts his left hand on the mat for base and uses the top of his left foot to push back against White's left thigh.

Blue pushes back with his left foot and pulls his right foot free.

Blue establishes the scarf hold position.

White catches Blue's right leg in the Half Guard.

Blue underhooks White's head with his left arm and walks his right foot toward White's hips. At the same time, Blue begins to push White's left inside knee outward to loosen the hold on his leg.

Blue pulls his right knee above White's legs and turns face down over White, pushing his knee to the mat.

Blue underhooks White's left arm with his right so that White cannot push Blue's knee. At the same time, Blue hooks the top of his left foot over the top of White's right thigh.

Blue pushes down with his left hook and pulls his right foot free.

Keeping his hips low and hugging White's neck tightly, Blue slides his feet onto the mat, establishing the top mount.

From his Half Guard, White crosses his ankles and hooks under Blue's right foot with his left foot. White straightens his legs for a calf crush.

Keeping his left knee close to White' side, Blue arches his torso upward and pushes down on White's chest with both hands.

Blue hooks the top of his right foot over the top of White's left foot, bends his left knee and comes to a standing position.

◉ This one is painful for both players, but it is worse for the guy on the bottom.

Blue stretches his left leg back for base, and drives White's feet up close to his rear with his right leg.

Blue brings his left foot back up parallel with his right, and stands up straight. By straightening his right leg, Blue crushes White's left calf against his own right shin.

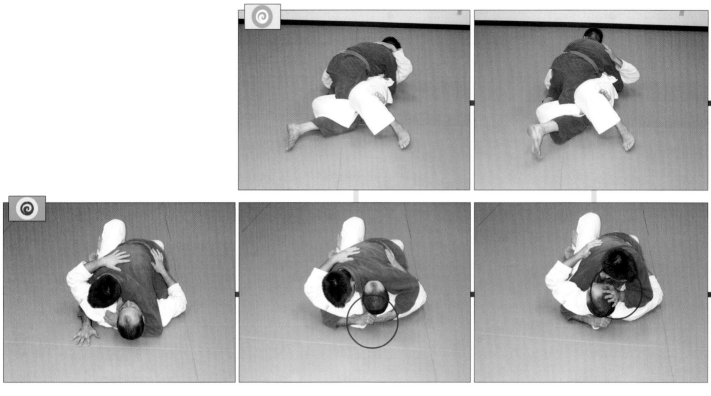

Blue has his right leg caught in White's half guard. Blue hooks his right arm underneath White's left.

Blue feeds White's collar from his left hand to his right.

Blue pushes White's head to the other side.

Blue now twists his hips to his left and begins to slide his right knee across the top of White's hips.

Blue pushes his right leg through to the mat on White's right side.

Blue lowers his head and presses the back of his head against the side of White's face.

Blue posts on the balls of his feet and raises his hips. Blue keeps pressure on White's upper body. Blue reaches back with his left hand and grabs White's right leg.

Blue pushes the leg downward. At the same time he twists his hips and starts to drive his right knee forward. Blue will drive his leg through forcefully, utilizing gravity and his weight to do so.

Blue pulls his right knee through and pushes White's knee with his left foot. Blue frees his right foot. Blue simultaneously pulls upward on White's right arm to keep White from turning.

Blue scissors his right leg forward and establishes control.

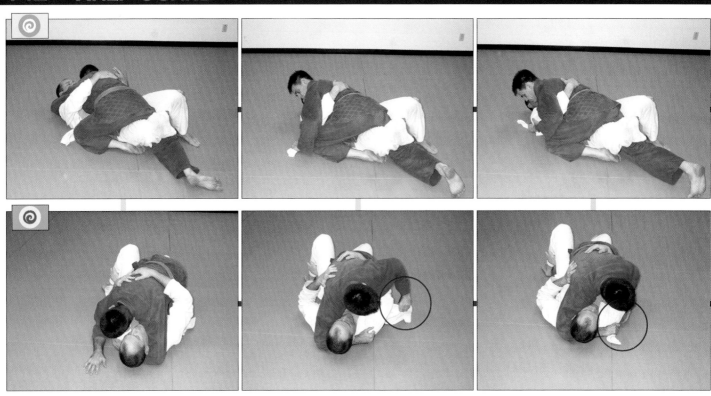

Blue's right leg is trapped in White's half guard. Blue has control of White's head.

Blue switches the arm controlling White's head. Blue grabs the bottom of white's right gi with his right hand.

Blue feeds the gi up and underneath White's right arm. Blue passes the cloth to his right hand, which is underneath White's neck. This traps White's head.

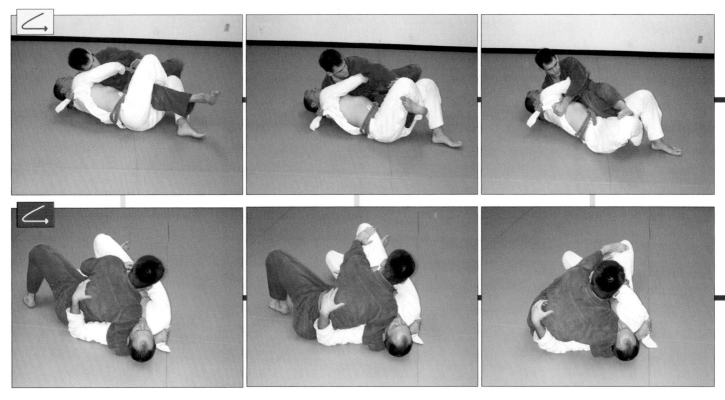

Blue now pushes inside White's right knee and begins to pull his right leg free. Notice Blue keeps tight control of White's neck with his right grip.

Blue pulls his right leg out as far as possible.

Blue pushes his left foot inside White's right knee so that he can pull his right foot free.

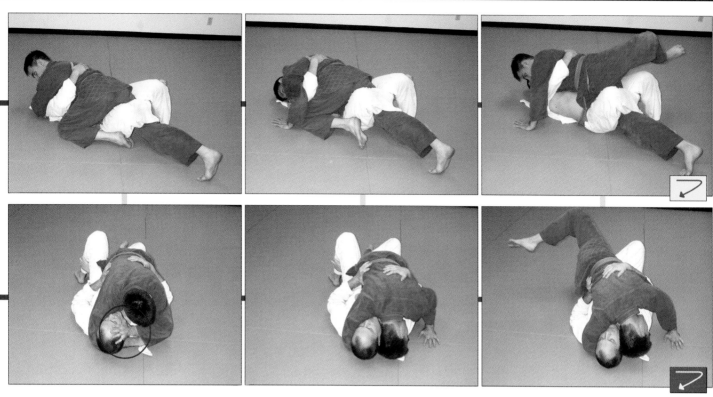

Blue pushes White's head to his left.

Blue lowers his head to the right side of White's head and posts his left hand for base.

Blue pushes off the mat with his left hand and swings his left leg back to White's left side.

Blue pulls his right foot free and puts the foot on the mat outside White's left hip.

❷ Blue never releases his grip on White's gi. The hold is crucial so that White cannot roll over on Blue while Blue is positioned to his side.

Blue twists his hips to his right and moves into side control.

◀▶White inserts his left leg between Blue's legs to close the half guard.

◀▶Blue underhooks White's thigh with one arm and hugs around White's waist with the other.

◀▶Blue extends his hips and straightens his legs. Blue crosses his ankles below White's ankle and pushes his hips forward, causing pressure against White's knee with his hips. When applying the kneebar, be sure that your hips are above your opponent's knee (never below) and that his knee faces directly into your torso. He pulls with his arms to keep things tight.

White has his right leg inserted between Blue's legs, and is about to close his Half Guard.

Blue quickly underhooks White's left leg with his right arm, preventing White from locking his legs.

Blue lifts his torso up, twists his hips to his right and slides his left knee across the top of White's hips. At the same time, Blue begins to slide his right arm toward White's ankle.

Blue slides his left knee under the outside of White's thigh as he lays on the mat beside White (it is important to lay parallel and not perpendicular to the opponent). Blue pinches his thighs together and hugs around White's ankle. Blue now arches his back pushing his pelvis forward for the kneebar.

CHAPTER 6

ATTACKS WHILE INSIDE THE GUARD

Although the dominate strategy while inside an opponent's Guard is to pass, there are times when attacking the opponent from inside the Guard is advisable. In chapter 3 we saw two choke attacks used primarily to open the legs. This chapter begins with another choking technique and then neckcranks. The focus of the chapter, however, is leg attacks.

There are three major types of leg attack from inside the Guard: straight foot locks, knee bars and toe holds. There are several variations of the straight foot lock, and it is the most commonly seen attack from inside the Guard. In competition, knee bars and toe holds are usually only allowed from the Purple belt level and above.

In order to attack the opponent's legs from the Guard, you must first open his legs, that is, you must break the closed Guard. Once the opponent's legs are open, the opportunity to attack is created. Successful leg attacks from the Guard are primarily dependent on proper timing, as the strength of the legs usually prohibits 'forcing' a technique. The position and movement of the opponent's legs as he works his open Guard will determine the types of leg attacks possible.

Foot locks are commonly done by securing the opponent's foot behind your armpit and then falling to the mat, either straight back or to the side. Most straight foot locks are done with the opponent's leg trapped between your legs, so it is important to bring a knee up between the opponent's legs as you fall back. Foot locks can also be done by turning the opponent over onto his face. The opponent's leg position will dictate opportunity. Note that foot locks are difficult to

finish if the opponent has a grip on your upper body, as he will be able to ride up as you fall, preventing you from stretching his leg and foot. Knee bars from the Guard are of the 'spinning' variety - meaning you need to turn the body 180 degrees to set up the leverage. It is possible to set up the knee bar from between the opponent's legs by spinning outward or from outside the opponent's legs by spinning inward. As for the foot lock, you must trap your opponent's leg between your legs to secure the hold. Unlike the foot lock, the knee bar can be set up from either an overhook or underhook grip on the leg.

The toe hold requires you to turn back toward the and secure a figure four grip around the foot and ankle. The resulting leverage is similar to a foot lock, but the foot is twisted inward as it is stretched. Since the toe hold is usually applied without the opponent's leg trapped between your legs, you must have a good grip on the foot and ankle with the opponent's foot held tightly to your chest to successfully apply the hold.

White hugs Blue around the body and pulls him down chest to chest. Blue underhooks White's head with his right arm.

This technique is an exception to the rule of thumb that you need position before submission. Beware of sweeps when attempting this one as you tend to tie your own hands up. If you have it deep enough, however, it will work from the bottom even after being swept.

Blue grabs inside his left sleeve with the four fingers of his right hand.

Though it is illegal to grab the end of your opponent's sleeve, it is permissible to do so to your own. Here it is necessary. Grap inside with four fingers for maximum power.

Blue moves his left hand over in a chopping motion on top of White's throat.

In this variation Blue uses his fist instead of the edge of his hand.

Blue pulls his left sleeve with his right hand as he presses the knife edge of his left hand down across White's throat for a sleeve choke.

White sits up in the Open Guard.

!Be extra cautious with any submissions involving the spinal column! The potential for serious injury must be taken seriously. It is one thing to hyperextend an elbow, and quite another to damage the spine!

Blue leans his weight forward, overhooks White's left arm with his right and reaches under White's right arm with his left. Sometimes it helps to push the head under the armpit with the opposite arm then underhook with the pushing hand *(see opposing page)*.

Hugging tightly, Blue steps out to his right with his right foot.

Blue moves his left foot across and drops his weight, sitting at White's left side. It is very important to keep hugging tightly and to keep the left elbow locked down so that the opponent cannot pop his head out from under the left armpit.

Blue puts his palm down on the mat both for base and to generate leverage to the back of his shoulder.

Blue scissors his left foot through to the front and hugging tightly with his arms, Blue leans back, applying pressure behind White's head with the back of his left shoulder. White's chin is forced to his chest in a neck crank submission.

This is a variation of the preceding technique. White sits up in his Open Guard.

Blue pushes on the back of White's head with his right hand, pushing the head under his left armpit.

Blue goes **under** White's left arm in this variation. On the preceding technique he went **over** White's arm.

Blue underhooks both of White's arms.

Blue steps to the side with his right foot.

Blue scissors his left leg through to the front and leans back for the neck crank.

▲ This is an alternative way to finish the technique. Instead of scissoring the left leg through to the front, you sprawl back both feet and post your palms on the mat. Push up off the mat and arch back for the neck crank submission.

◀▶Blue stands in White's open guard.

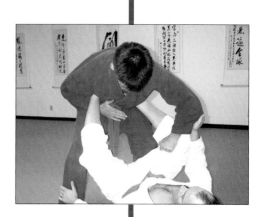

◀▶Blue wraps his right arm tightly around White's right ankle, and pushes White's right leg with his other hand.

◀▶Blue moves his left leg in between White's legs and falls back to the mat. As he sits back, Blue pinches his legs together tightly to isolate White's left leg. Blue allows his right arm to slide down White's leg until this wrist is below White's Achilles' tendon (just above the heel).

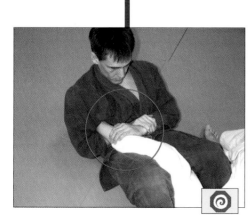

◀▶Blue then makes a figure four lock by grabbing over the top of his left wrist with his right hand as he grabs over the top of White's shin with his left hand. Keeping his elbows pulled back and in, Blue lifts his chest and arches his back, pulling up under White's Achilles' tendon and stretching the top of White's foot back for the submission.

White turns to his right side and slides his left shin across Blue's hips in the scissors sweep position.

Blue keeps his hips down, and pushes inside Blue's right knee with his left palm, pinning White's right leg to the mat. At the same time, Blue begins to wrap White's right ankle with his right arm.

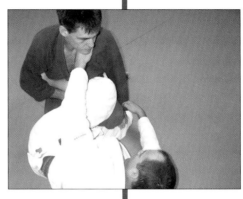

Blue slides his left knee over the top of White's right thigh, and falls onto his left side.

A basic defense for White would be to grab Blue by the lapels, behind his head, or over his shoulder. That would allow him to pull himself ontop of Blue and push his foot through or put the sole of his foot on the floor. Obviously then, it is better that Blue keep himself out of reach or that he breack White's grip before making his attack.

Blue locks his hands in a figure four around White's ankle and begins to bring his left foot over White's left leg.

Blue puts his right foot on the mat, squeezes his legs tightly and arches his back while pulling up under White's ankle for the submission.

USING THE FEET

Blue sets up the footlock. Blue squeezes White's left leg between his legs and wraps his right arm around Blue's left ankle. Blue pushes White's left hip with his right foot to keep him from sitting up and defending the hold. Blue figure fours his hands grabbing his left wrist with his right palm and putting his left palm on top of White's shin.

Blue squeezes his knees together, locks his elbows back tight to his own body, lifts his right wrist upward into White's Achilles' tendon. Blue lifts his chest and leans back his head as he arches back. He uses his torso to generate the power for the footlock, not just his arms.

Blue sets up the footlock with a leg scissors hold. Blue crosses his right leg over the top of White's left thigh.

❷ To be good at ankle locks, you need to be good at controlling your opponent with your legs. Putting your feet on his hips or the inside of his thigh generally works.

Here White keeps White at a distance by controlling the inside of Blue's leg with his foot. Note also how Blue has triangled his legs. This is to help make more pressure for the submission.

Blue tightens his grip around White's ankle as he rolls onto his left side and hooks his right foot behind his left knee. Blue's left foot pushes the inside of White's right knee to prevent White from sitting up.

OPPOSITE HANDS

In this variation of the above grip, Blue inserts his left wrist under White's left ankle, grabs his right biceps with his left palm and makes a figure four grip.

Blue arches back and pulls his left wrist up under White's ankle to finish the footlock.

LAPEL GRIP

An alternate grip for the footlock. Blue inserts his right wrist under White's left ankle, and grabs his lapel to lock White's ankle. Blue uses his other hand to pull on his opposite lapel. That keeps the arm locking the foot from slipping along with the lapel.

White sets up the De La Riva Guard with his right foot inserted between Blue's legs from the rear, and hooked over the top of Blue's right leg.

Blue turns to his right, pivoting on his left foot and swinging his right foot back a step. As he turns, Blue hooks his right arm under White's right ankle and grabs his left lapel to secure the leg.

Blue sits down as close as possible to White's right hip, and wraps his left arm around White's leg.

Blue falls back parallel to White's leg. He simultaneously crosses his ankles and squeezes his legs together tightly.

Hugging White's leg tightly to his chest, Blue arches his back and pushes his hips forward for a kneebar submission.

◄► Blue is passing White's Open Guard, and has White's right leg underhooked with his left arm. Blue holds outside White's left knee with the dual purpose of immobilizing White and providing base for himself.

◄► Blue twists his hips and swings his right foot over White's right leg, putting his foot down outside White's right hip. Blue hugs White's leg close to his chest with his left arm.

◄► Blue sits straight down on the top of White's right hip.

◄► Blue falls back on the mat at White's right side, hugging his leg tightly. Blue squeezes White's thigh with his legs and arches his hips for the kneebar.

◀▶ Blue is passing White's open guard. Blue wraps his left arm over the top of White's right leg.

◀▶ Blue slides his right knee through but allows his foot to hook the top of White's thigh. Blue posts with his right arm for base and to aid in the transition to the mat.

◀▶ Blue lays on the mat, supporting himself on his right elbow. Blue pulls his elbow back as he squeezes his legs and pushes his hips forward for the kneebar. The movement of the hips is similar to a straight arm armbar.

◀ Blue finishes the move by straightening his body. Everything must be tight before he straightens out.

Blue is passing White's Open Guard.

Blue pivots, pulls White's right leg up and underhooks White's right ankle with his right arm.

Blue squats and presses his left knee on top of White's right hip.

Blue falls back parallel with White's leg. He squeezes White's right thigh between his legs as he hugs the leg tightly.

The finish from a different angle.

White holds Blue in the De La Riva guard position with his right leg inserted between Blue's legs from the rear and the top of his right foot hooked over the front of Blue's right hip. White grabs Blue's belt with his right hand from the rear. White will pull Blue's belt back with is right hand attempting to sweep Blue to the rear.

As White pulls back with his right hand and pushes back with his right leg, Blue follows the momentum and turns his body to the right, pivoting on his left foot as he swings his right foot back. Blue hooks his right arm under White's right ankle as he turns.

As always, **BE CAREFUL**. It is easy to hurt someone's knee or pop a tendon in their ankle with this one. With leg attacks physical damage has a way of happening before the submission is very painful.

Blue grabs over the top of White's right foot with his left hand, thumb facing his chest. Blue grabs just below White's toes at the top of his foot. Blue grabs the top of his left wrist with his right hand (his right wrist is wrapped under White's right ankle) in a figure four position.

Blue lowers his hips, pulls White's right foot toward his chest and simultaneously pushes down with both hands, twisting White's right foot in an inward spiral for the submission.
This one will lead to knee injuries if the foot is twisted rather than attacking the achilies tendon.

❂ There is an argument to be made that this technique violates the prohibition against techninques which twist the knee. For the most part, however, it is allowed in competition between higher belts.

CHAPTER 7

TURTLE POSITION

The Turtle position usually occurs when you are attempting to pass the Guard and your opponent back rolls to his knees to prevent you from gaining scoring points. If your opponent back rolls to his knees as you pass, you will have an advantage, but no points will be scored. The danger to the opponent is that he will expose his back to attack, if only momentarily.

As soon as the opponent rolls back to the all fours position, you need to prevent him from either controlling your legs for a single or double leg takedown, or sitting back to his Guard. You need to move to maintain your advantageous position. The best way to maintain control of the opponent who rolls back to the Turtle position is to first crush him with your weight and then control his head and/or limbs. You may use your chest of one of your hands for this initial control. Without first putting some weight on the opponent's upper back or head, it will be very difficult to control his movement.

Once your opponent rolls into the Turtle position, you can control him from a couple different positions as you prepare to attack.

1. You can control the opponent from the side position – facing the same way as the opponent with your close knee under the opponent's chest and your outside leg posted on the mat for stability (i.e. pg. 160).

2. You can control from the head to head position – facing the opponent's feet with your chest pressing down on the back of the opponent's head and upper back (i.e. pg. 174).

In each of these positions the arms and legs will also be used to control the opponent in various ways: wrist control, hugging the back, locking the head, wrapping the arms, wrapping the legs, etc…. The control position you adopt will dictate the kinds of offensive techniques and submissions available to you.

Once you are controlling your opponent in the Turtle position, there are a large variety of submissions available. You can attack the opponent's arms, setting up armbars, shoulder locks and keylocks. You can attack the opponent's neck with chokes and strangles. You can attack the legs as well. In addition to submission techniques, it is also possible to force the opponent into other disadvantageous positions. With the opponent controlled in the Turtle position, you can take the back, putting your hooks in for points as you set up submission techniques. You can break the opponent down flat on his stomach and then attack. You can also turn the opponent onto his back, coming into the side control position.

Most of the techniques shown in this chapter begin with the opponent to the side rather than head to head. It is relatively easy to rotate from a head to head position to a side by side position. It is also relatively easy to switch from one side to the other. Whatever the transition, be mindful to keep some weight on your opponent. Most attacks from the head to head situation are chokes. Look for openings for a choke whenever in this position. If there are none, move to the side.

Take advantage of the turtle position when your opponent gives it. It is a bad position for him. As the chapter illustrates, there are many opportunities to attack for the player on top.

White back rolls out of the Guard and goes to his hands and knees in the turtle position. Blue grabs four fingers inside White's rear collar with his left hand and holds the back of White's belt with his right hand. Blue presses his right knee in between White's left elbow and knee and posts his left foot out for base.

Blue lifts up on White to make space to slide his right knee under White's chest and then Blue drops his weight onto White's back.

Blue reaches his right hand under White's right armpit and grabs White's right collar with his right hand.

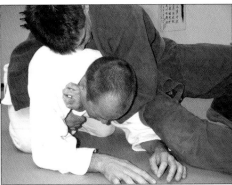

In this variation, instead of grabbing White's wrist with his right hand, Blue grabs White's left lapel for control. This increases the action of the choke but decreases Blue's control of White.

Blue scissors his right leg through to the front.

Blue thrusts his hips forward and pulls his left elbow back to complete the choke.

Reaching above White's left arm, Blue slides his left wrist across the front of White's throat and grabs inside White's right collar with a thumb in grip as far behind the neck as possible.

Blue now lets go of White's lapel with his right hand and grabs White's right wrist for wrist control.

Blue scissors his left foot through to the front and moves around the front of White's head while pulling his left elbow back to finish White with the Clock Choke. Blue sits his weight onto White's shoulder and pulls the opposite direction. Note how Blue lifts his shoulder.

In this variation of the Clock Choke, Blue obtains the cross collar grips.

Blue lowers his left knee and shoulder toward the mat.

Blue posts his head on the mat and pulls outward strongly with both hands for the submission.

FEEDING THE GI

Use one hand to make it easy for the other to get a deep grip. The idea is to make space for an easy entry. Feeding the gi from one hand to another is key to many techniques.

Blue feeds White's left collar to his right hand (the right arm must be above White's right arm).

Blue pulls the slack out of the cloth with his left hand and grabs as far up the collar with his right hand as he can.

Blue attempts to set up the Clock Choke, grabbing inside White's lapel with his right hand. White pulls down on Blue's arm and blocks the grip of the second hand.

Maintaining his grip on the collar, Blue stands and pushes down on the back of White's head with his left hand, preventing White from escaping the position.

Blue steps his right leg over the top of White's head.

Blue attempts the above technique, but White grabs around his right leg for a single leg takedown.

The position from a different angle.

Blue grabs White's rear belt with his left hand.

Blue twists a bit to make things tighter.

Blue pulls upward with his right hand so that his wrist bone cuts into the right side of White's neck as he simultaneously straightens his right leg, squeezing his calf into the left side of White's neck for the strangle.

⊙ Variation: Blue slides his right shin across the back of Blue's neck behind his right arm. Blue then pushes down with his shin and pulls up with his right arm for the strangle.

Blue presses his left shin behind White's left shoulder.

Blue falls back and extends his right leg straight over the back of White's head, hooking his foot underneath White's left armpit.

Controlling Blue with his right leg and left grip, Blue pulls with his right arm and pushes with the back of his leg for the choke.

Rolling Clock Choke. Blue sets up the Clock Choke. Blue has a right grip, thumb in, inside White's left collar. Blue reaches underneath White's left arm with his left.

Blue does a forward roll over White's left shoulder.

The roll flips White over onto his back.

White bridges ontop of Blue.

White back rolls over Blue, attempting to escape the choke.

Blue maintains his grips and rolls up with White.

Blue slides his hips away from White's head, while maintaining his grips.

Blue scissors his left leg back under his right.

Blue turns to his belly, at the same time pulling with his right arm, increasing the pressure of the choke. It is important to maintain the left grip around the opponent's left arm with your left so that he cannot turn out of the choke. Blue uses his shoulder to make pressure also.

Blue comes up on his knees and drives his left knee underneath White.

The finishing position from the opposite angle.

Blue is in position to submit White with the basic Clock Choke.

White is in the turtle position. Blue kneels at White's right side and holds over White's back with his left arm. Blue reaches underneath White's chest with his right arm, grabbing around the outside of White's left upper arm.

Blue reaches his left arm in front of White's right thigh, and reaches under White to grab his left ankle.

Blue lifts his knees, pushes off the balls of his feet while pulling with his hands. The pressure rolls White onto his back (Blue's grips prevents White from posting his left arm or leg to stop the movement).

The position from another angle.

Blue brings his knees up and establishes side control.

This variation starts from the same position. Blue reaches underneath White's chest and grabs around his left upper arm with his right hand.

Blue reaches his left arm underneath White's chest and grabs around the other side of White's left upper arm.

Blue lifts his knees and drives forward off the balls of his feet as he pulls in on White's left arm.

Blue rolls White onto his back.

White goes to the turtle position. Blue drives his left knee underneath White's chest. Blue holds the back of White's collar with his right hand and the back of White's belt with his left hand. Blue keeps his weight pressing down on White's back.

White steps his right foot over White's right forearm and slides the arm out.

Blue pulls White's right arm back straight with his right leg.

Blue crosses his ankles underneath White's wrist, straightens his legs and presses down with his hips for an armbar (it is important to trap the opponent's arm with the back of the elbow facing upward).

From the previous technique, White counters the armbar by bending his elbow and moving his hand upward.

Blue changes his base by twisting his hips forward as he reaches over White's back with his left arm. Blue slides his left knee on the mat close to White's side.

Blue scissors his left knee underneath White. He sits on his hip and twists back, cranking White's right arm. The submission is an American lock variation.

White twists his right arm back to avoid the straight armbar.

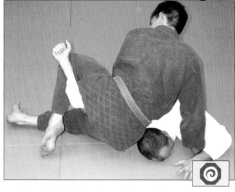

Blue bends his left leg back to trap the arm and twists his hips so his right thigh slides under White's shoulder. Be sure to keep your hips over the back of the opponent's shoulders with the weight down so the opponent cannot roll forward. The result is a chicken-wing type shoulder lock.

Blue traps White's arm between his legs as in the preceding teschniques. Blue grabs underneath White's neck with his right arm, and reaches over White's back with his left arm.

With White in the Turtle position, Blue drives his left knee underneath White's chest. At the same time, Blue hugs White's back with his left arm and controls White's right shoulder with his right grip.

Blue twists his hips to his right and uses his left knee to slide White's right arm away from his body.

Blue quickly steps his right foot over the top of White's right arm and hooks the wrist.

▲▼Blue grabs inside White's left collar with his right hand, thumb in. Blue then underhooks White's left arm with his left, and secures the grip by grabbing his own right lapel.

Blue turns his head to his right and rolls over White's back, turning White face up.

Blue holds White in the Crucifix position. Blue controls White's left arm with his left and pulls with his right arm to choke White.

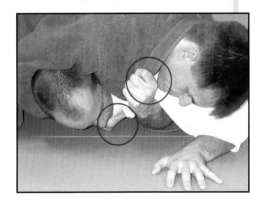

Blue scissors White's right arm and inserts his left hand below White's left arm for wrist control.

Blue pushes off the mat with his left foot and rolls over White's back, turning White face up in the Crucifix position. Blue grabs his own lapel with his left hand to secure White's left arm.

Blue pulls with his right arm to choke White. Blue's left hand releases White's wrist and switches to help apply pressure to White's neck to finish the choke.

Blue takes wrist control with his left hand and slides his right shin behind White's neck. Blue Then pushes forward with his right shin and pulls with his left arm to complete the choke. You may need to make a small snake (hip) movement to make space to get your leg behind the neck

Blue has completed the roll and holds White in the Crucifix position. Blue can submit White in various ways.

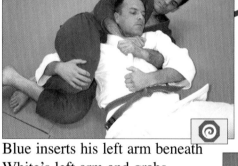

Blue inserts his left arm beneath White's left arm and grabs White's right lapel. Blue then pulls back with his right arm as he pushes down with his left hand to complete the choke.

Blue reaches through below White's left armpit and holds his lapel.

Blue then slides his left hand down behind White's neck in a chopping motion (leading with the little finger) as he simultaneously pulls back with his right arm to finish the choke.

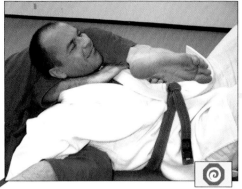

Blue maintains the grip on White's left collar with his right hand. Blue then brings his right leg up and over White's head and hooks the back of his right knee on the left side of White's head. Blue pulls back with his right leg and simultaneously pulls with his right arm to finish the choke.

The choke from another angle.

Blue keeps his right leg hooked tightly around White's right arm, and he reaches his right arm over the top of White's left arm.

Keeping his hips low behind White's neck, Blue twists his body to the left, forcing White's chin to his chest for a neck crank.

Blue grabs his own lapel with his left arm to secure White's left arm.

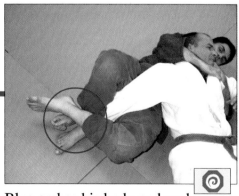

Blue arches his body and pushes down with his legs to stretch out White's right arm for shoulder and elbow pressure.

White is in the turtle position. Blue controls from the top holding White's neck and belt with his weight over White's upper back. White grabs inside Blue's left leg to set up a single leg takedown.

Blue grabs white's right wrist with his left hand. At the same time, Blue turns his body back to his right so that he is parallel to White's body.

Blue posts his right hand and begins to lower his body.

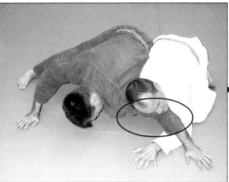

Blue is controlling White from the side, with his left knee under White's chest and his left arm hugging White's back. White reaches back with his right arm in an attempt to control Blue's left leg (White's idea is to sit up and lift Blue's leg forward, which will throw Blue onto his back).

To prevent Blue from lifting his leg, Blue lowers his torso and reaches across the front of White's neck. Posting his left hand outside White's left arm. White cannot lift Blue's leg from this position.

Blue turns his head to look to his right and rolls forward over his left shoulder

Blue turns his head to his right and rolls over his left shoulder.

Blue rolls up to the sitting position. As Blue rolls, he hooks his left leg back to trap White's right arm behind his knee. As Blue sits up, he pulls White's wrist outside his left hip.

Blue immediately reaches over White's back to stop him from rolling over out of the shoulder lock. Blue has White in the omo plata.

If White does not tap, Blue moves both feet to his right for base and lifts his hips upward and forward toward White's head. He scoops up White's free arm and pulls it toward him. White taps (with his feet).

Blue keeps his arm across White's body.

The roll flips White over onto his back.

Blue rolls up to a sitting position and triangles his leg, trapping White's right arm. Blue still controls underneath White's left arm. White is prevented from sitting up. By pulling back with his legs and upping his hips, Blue will crank White's elbow or shoulder.

If White does not submit, Blue turns and comes to his knees for side control.

White is in the Turtle position. Blue sprawls on the back of his head. Blue holds inside White's belt at the rear center with his left hand palm up. Blue uses the belt as a fulcrum and pushes down on White's back with his left elbow to hold White down. Blue is also holding the back of White's collar with his right hand for control.

Blue inserts his right arm under White's left arm while keeping his weight down.

Keeping the grip of the belt, Blue grabs his left wrist with his right, figure four style.

Blue holds White in the same position as above.

Blue underhooks White's left arm with his right arm and grabs his own left wrist.

Blue brings his knees up and sits on the back of White's head.

Blue brings his knees up and sits on the back of White's head, pinching White's head between his knees.

The position from the opposite side.

Blue begins to twist to his left, driving his left knee into White's side as he pulls up on White's left arm.

Blue falls back, trapping White's head below his right leg as he brings his left knee up behind White's left armpit.

Blue finishes with an armbar

Blue now grabs his own left lapel with his right hand, locking White's left arm to his chest. Blue posts his left palm on the mat for base and turns to his right.

Blue continues turning to his right as he slides his left knee over White's back. Blue lowers his left hip to the mat and slides his left knee underneath White's left arm. Blue's right shin pushes against the left side of White's head.

Blue pinches his knees and pushes his legs forward as he arches his back, pulling White's left arm straight into an armbar.

White is in the Turtle Position. Blue sits over the back of White's head and grabs the back of White's belt with his left hand for control. Blue begins to reach under White's left arm with his right hand.

Blue turns his body to the left and inserts his right arm through White's left armpit.

Blue falls to his back at White's left side. Blue maintains his grip on the back of White's belt with his left hand, and he grabs his own left wrist with his right hand.

White is in the Turtle Position. Blue holds from the side.

Blue works his hands in under White's armpits and grabs White's wrists.

Blue moves around to White's rear and sits low on White's hips.

White is in the Turtle Position. Blue holds from the side.

Blue moves around to White's rear and sits low on his hips. Blue grabs inside White's rear collar with both hands.

Blue begins to pull back on White's collar.

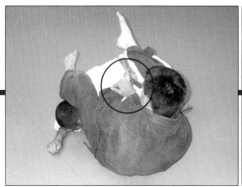

Blue holds down White's head with his left leg and begins to move his right leg over the top of White's right arm.

Blue locks his feet and squeezes his knees around White's left arm.

Blue grabs his left biceps with his right hand, turning his wrist so the wrist bones press into White's biceps and forearm. Blue extends his legs and simultaneously pulls his left wrist toward himself for a keylock on White's left elbow.

Blue leans back, lifting White up.

Blue puts his hooks in (note Blue is lifting up under White's arms so he cannot block the hooks).

Blue falls to his side and pulls White over, taking White's back.

Blue pulls White up and pinches White's sides with his knees.

Blue puts both hooks in.

Blue falls back to his side, taking White's back.

With a grip secure (*see below*), Blue sprawls back and puts weight over the back of White's head.

Blue begins to twist his right side down to the mat.

Blue lays on his right side, scissors his right leg through and begins to duck his head underneath White's left armpit.

Blue continues to roll over to his left side, rolling White over his head while turning White onto his back.

Once White is on his back and Blue's head is clear, Blue begins to backroll over on top of White. Blue rolls over his shoulder, not his head.

▲▼Blue lands in the top mount position. Blue now twists his body to the right and pulls with his right hand for a choke.

Close up of the grip: Blue is over White's head. Blue grabs White's right lapel with his left hand, thumb in and reaches underneath White's left arm with his right hand.

Blue feeds White's left collar to his right hand, gripping with four fingers inside the lapel.

Blue now grabs his own right wrist with his left hand.

Blue holds inside White's right lapel with his left hand, while keeping his weight sprawled on White's upper back.

Blue reaches underneath White's left armpit with his right hand and grabs inside White's right collar with a four finger grip.

Blue now grabs the back of White's collar with is left hand, thumb in.

The hold from a different angle.

Blue lowers his left elbow toward the mat and moves his feet back.

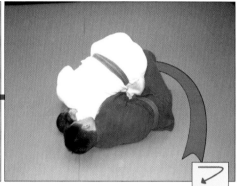

Blue scissors his left leg across below his right leg and lays on his left side right next to White's left leg (as close as possible).

Blue twists toward his right, pulling White over the top of his chest.

White lands on his back at Blue's right side.

Blue continues turning to his right and comes to his knees. Blue pulls with his right hand as he simultaneously pushes his left elbow downward to finish the choke.

See also the variation on the next page.

White is in the Turtle Position. Blue lays across White's shoulders and holds over his back with his left arm. Blue grabs White's right lapel with is left hand and feeds the collar to his right hand (Blue reaches his right hand underneath White's neck).

Blue Grabs inside White's right lapel with his right hand, four fingers inside the lapel.

Blue grabs White's right elbow with his left hand.

❷ This technique is a variation on the one from the preceding page. Here instead of going on his back, Blue is able to set the choke by focusing his weight into his forearm and keeping it there. The action of Blue's leg stepping under and through is similar for both techniques.

After Blue has his right grip in place (Blue reaches behind White's left arm and grabs four fingers inside White's right lapel), he grabs the back of White's collar with his left hand, thumb in.

Blue twists his hips to the right and drops his left hip toward the mat as he pulls with his right hand and pushes his left elbow downward for the choke.

Blue pulls White's right arm back under White's head to break his base. Blue simultaneously moves his hips around the top of White's head (Blue shuffles his feet to his left).

Blue twists to his right, laying his left side on the mat as he ducks his head underneath White's right armpit. He scissors his legs as he rolls.

Blue continues to roll to his right, pulling White over his chest.

With White flat on his back and Blue's head clear, Blue scissors his feet.

Blue continues to turn until he is face down. Blue slides his left arm behind White's head for control and pulls with his right to finish the choke.

After the roll, Blue can also secure White's right arm by gripping behind his shoulder.

Blue twists face down and pulls with his right hand to finish the choke.

❷ This attack is somewhat unorthodox. As a result, White is unprepared for the attack on his neck.

White goes to the Turtle Position. Controlling from the side, Blue reaches under both of White's armpits and grabs the lapels on both sides. Blue drives his weight into White with his posted right foot.

Blue quickly slides his right knee in close to White's right knee, and simultaneously swings his left knee behind White's rear.

Blue leans back and using his weight, pulls White onto his right side. As Blue pulls back, he swings his left leg around to his rear for base.

Posting on his left foot, Blue scissors his right leg back and underneath his left.

Blue comes to the sprawl position behind White's head.

Blue moves back away from White and pulls White flat onto his back. Pushing off the balls of his feet, Blue now drives his right shoulder into the back of White's head to force his chin to his chest, resulting in a forward neck crank.

Continuing from the North/South sprawl control, Blue reaches around White's neck with his right hand and grabs thumb inside White's left lapel, as high up as possible.

Blue now comes to his knees and turns White onto his right side. Blue releases his left lapel grip and slides his left arm up behind White's neck.

Blue chops down with his left hand as he pulls with his right hand to apply the single wing choke.

This is another finish from the same position. Blue grips White's left collar with his right hand, thumb in. Blue then reaches straight across with his left hand and grabs White's right lapel, thumb in.

Blue moves to his left and pulls down with his left hand as he pulls back with his right for the sliding collar choke. Blue does not keep his chest tight. To the contrary, he makes space.

Continuing from the previous position, Blue can also set up the armbar. Blue grabs his own lapel with his left hand. Blue grabs inside White's right lapel with his right hand, and brings his arm in front of White's throat. Blue pushes down with his weight into his right arm to pin Blue to the mat on his side.

Keeping his hips low, Blue swings his right leg over White's head.

Sitting as close as possible to White's shoulder and pinching his knees tight, Blue falls back for the armbar.

White is in the Turtle Position, Blue controls from the side.

Blue pulls up on White's belt and collar and slips his right foot inside White's right leg as far as possible (Blue tries to press his right instep against the front of White's right hip).

A rear view of the position.

From the same position as above, Blue kicks his right leg inside White's right leg.

Blue bends his right knee forward to put pressure against White's right hip.

Blue 'walks' his right foot outward to create space between White's right leg and torso, to weaken his base.

Blue lowers his head and begins to turn his body to the left.

Blue posts his right hand on the mat for base, and begins to slide his left foot back under White's neck.

Blue lays down on his right side and continues twisting to his left as he slides his left leg underneath White's neck.

Switching his right grip to the belt, Blue grabs under White's right arm from the top with his left hand and swings his left foot back and around to his left until his back faces White's right side.

Blue pulls White's right arm up with his left arm and grabs his own right lapel to secure the arm.

Blue falls back over White to take the armbar.

Switching his right grip to hold White's belt, Blue swings his left leg back and around to his left so his back is facing White's right side.

Blue underhooks White's left arm with his left.

Blue bends forward and grabs his right lapel with his left hand, securing White's right arm.

Blue's shin is tight against White's face.

Blue extends his body and pushes his left shin up against the right side of White's head.

Blue lays flat, squeezes his knees tightly and arches his back for the armbar.

Blue begins the same as in the previous technique by slipping his right leg inside White's right leg. Note that Blue has already secured White's right arm with a left underhook.

Blue falls onto his left side, maintaining his left grip on the belt and his control of White's right arm.

Close up of the position.

Blue begins the same as the previous technique by slipping his right leg inside White's right leg.

Blue turns left, sliding his left foot back and around over the top of White's head.

Blue lowers his weight and controls White's upper body.

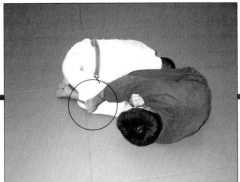

Blue grabs the cloth outside White's right ankle.

Even better: grab the foot near the toes if you can reach it.

Blue pulls White's right ankle outward and secures his right hook underneath White's right hip.

Blue pulls White's right leg outward then over his head.

As White flips over to his back, Blue moves his left leg over White's head to secure the armbar.

Rear view of the position.

White is so intent on not giving up his arm that he leaves space on his left side.

Blue continues turning to his left and slides his left foot back past White's left shoulder.

Blue slides his left hook inside White's left hip and hugs White's upper body. Blue now has both hooks inside White's hips and has taken White's back.

White is in the Turtle Position, Blue approaches from the side. Blue grabs the back of White's collar and belt. Blue pulls upward to make space to put his left hook inside White's left hip.

Blue now steps over White's back and hooks his right leg over the top of White's right shoulder.

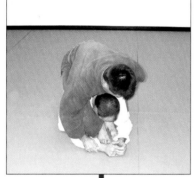

Blue hooks his right leg tightly underneath White's throat as he underhooks White's left arm with his left arm.

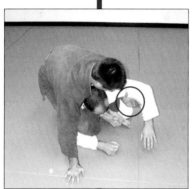

White falls onto his right side and pulls White on top of him. Notice how Blue pulls upward on White's left arm.

Blue triangles his legs by locking his right ankle behind his left knee. White is now caught in a back triangle

White is in the Turtle Position. Blue slides his left wrist underneath White's throat until the thumb side of his wrist is against White's trachea. Blue simultaneously presses the bottom of his left wrist on the back of White's neck. Blue keeps his weight down on the back of White's head.

Blue points the fingers of his right hand downward and locks his hands together in a palm to palm grip. Blue now squeezes his elbows together. He concetrates his weight into the blade of his forearm and into the back of White's neck.

❷ This technique can be set up two ways. The arm across the front of the throat can enter underneath White's armpit or in front of White's shoulder. The under the armpit technique fools some players because they assume that there is no choke that way... but there is!

CHAPTER 8

DRILLS

Solo grappling drills are an important part of training. Practicing solo drills confers two very important benefits. The first being an increase in the physical attributes required for competitive grappling: strength, speed, flexibility, balance, endurance and agility. These attributes are developed in a task specific manner, meaning exactly as they will be needed when actually grappling. Secondly, drills mimic techniques or aspects of techniques which are actually applied on opponents. Solo practice serves to reinforce correct technique in your muscle memory. The mind has to learn how the body moves, drills are a way of teaching it.

We all know that the best techniques in the world are useless if we are not in good enough shape to apply them. That being said, bear in the maxim that you can only cheat yourself when it comes to drills. Drills will help get you in shape while at the same time helping to develop correct movement skills for technique.

The drills in this chapter were selected wih passing the Guard in mind. Most of the drills shown involve hip and core body movement. Hip movement is key to Brazilian Jiu Jitsu (and indeed to many other martial arts and sports). Good hip movement is essential for actualizing a lot of the techniques in this book, especially the trickier ones.

When practicing look for ways to improve your body movement in terms of efficiency and smoothness. Work out kinks and rough spots. Smoothness requires relaxation and attention to the body's own signals.

At the end of the chapter are two partner drills. Those drills use the partner's weight or position as resistance. Like the solo drills, partner drills serve the dual purpose of conditioning and reinforcing correct movement. Drills, and especially partner drills can be created for virtually any technical movement, and are only limited by the practitioner's imagination and ingenuity.

Most techniques can be practiced as drills and repeating a specific technique over and over is a good drill. When practicing a technique for the first time your partner should not be resisting. Once you get the idea and are executing a new technique with some degree of proficientcy, have your partner offer increasing amounts of resistance.

Working on things in isolation, ultimately, is not sufficient. Try playing a game where one player resists 50% or so and the other makes from one to three moves. The players then switch so that so that the guy who was going half speed gives the other guy a chance to try his moves. Go back and forth. If both guys are not tapping, at least one is resisting too much. The idea is to work on transition, flow, and counters. You both must 'leave your egos at the door' to reap the benefits of this type of training. You do not need to restart everytime there is a submission. Instead, back off the submission and let the other guy begin his turn by making some sort of escape.

Enen though this type of training is cooperative, it can be quite vigorous. This type of training has the advantage of allowing you to attepmt moves in a dynamic situation without significant consequences for failure.

Lay on your back in the Guard position.

Lift your hips straight up as far as possible.

Turn onto your right shoulder and feed your right arm below your hip behind you as you post your left hand above your head.

Scissors your left foot over your right foot so that you are sprawling on your right shoulder (look to your left).

Kick both feet over your head.

Land on the soles of your feet. You will have turned 180 degrees from the starting position.

Repeat the drill again in the opposite direction by twisting toward your left shoulder, reaching your left arm underneath your body and over your head with your right hand.

Step your right leg over your left.

Posting on your left shoulder, kick both feet over your head.

Land on the soles of your feet in the original, starting position.

Start in a sprawl position.

Post on your right hand and scissor your right leg across to the left.

Post your right foot and twist your torso to the left, whipping your left hand back over to post on the mat even with your right hand.

Continuing, post on your right foot and thread the left leg back beneath your hips as you twist your body to the left.

Reach over with your right hand and post the hand on the ground in the sprawl position (your position will be rotated 90 degrees from the start position).

Repeat.

Strive for smoothness and fluidity.

Start in a squat position with both palms on the ground.

Scissor your right foot across the front of your body to the left.

Extend the right leg as far as possible as you twist the torso to the left.

Pull your hips back and begin to retract the leg.

Put your left hand back on the mat and bend your right leg underneath your body.

Return to the start position.

The drill should be done side to side in a fluid motion.

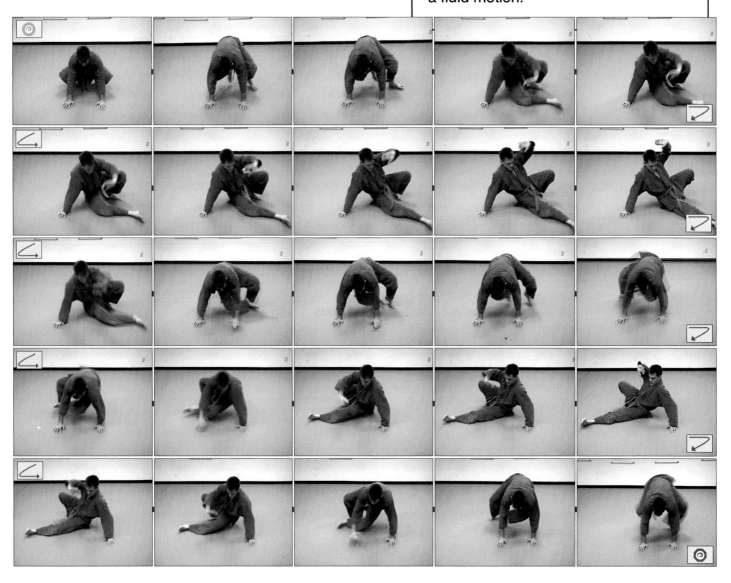

Start sitting on your knees with your fists or palms on the mat.

Lean forward and push your weight into your hands and hop both feet up to a low squat position (don't lift your hips any higher than necessary to get your feet underneath you).

Kick your feet back to a full sprawl position. Keep your head up, your arms locked straight, your shoulders pressed down and your pelvis to the mat. As you sprawl back, keep your hips as low as possible.

Hop the feet back up to the squat position.

Drop back down onto your knees.

Repeat.

Start kneeling with the top of your head on the mat. Put your palms on the mat on either side of your head.

Straighten your legs and post on your toes. Your torso should be vertical with the weight distributed between the top of your head and your hands.

Kick both feet over your head and arch your back.

Land on the soles of your feet in a back arch position (head off the mat).

This is the complete drill in motion sequence. After landing on the feet in the back arch position, twist to one side and roll to the knees.

Lay face down with the arms extended out to the sides, look to your left.

Whip your left leg back over to your right, putting the sole of the foot on the mat. Try to open the pelves and point your left knee straight at the ceiling.

Return to the starting position and turn your head to look to the right.

Repeat to the other side. Try to trace a high arching path with your legs.

▼ **Handstand to the sprawl position.** Put your hands down ahead of your body ad kick one foot then the other straight up over your head to the handstand position. Slowly bend your arms and lower your chest to the mat. Keep your back arched and roll down the front of your body until your legs are on the mat. Let the momentum carry your upper body up and push with your arms into the sprawl position (you should have a spotter catch your feet and help balance you in the handstand position when first learning the drill).

This is a drill that builds explosive strength from sitting on the feet. This movement is useful when jumping up to the standing position from the Guard. It also builds coordination between the upper and lower body.

Sit on the heels. Begin by swinging your arms over head to help lift the weight of your upper body off your legs. As you hips begin to rise, contract your abs and pull your knees up toward your chest. Pull your feet up under your hips and land in the full squat position.

❷ Variation: You can make the exercise more challenging by rotating your body 90 degrees in the air as you spring up.

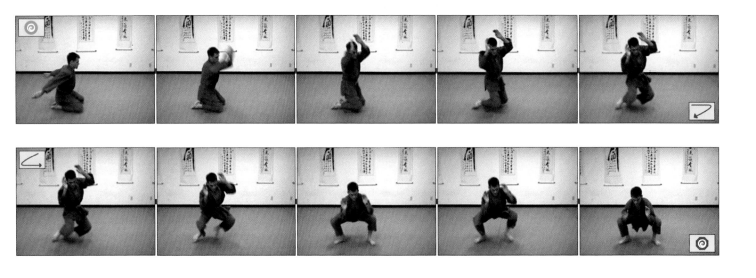

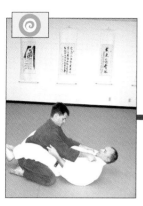    

Sit in your partner's Closed Guard. Grab both lapels high up on your partner's collar.

Stand up.

Keeping your back straight, squat a little and arch back, lifting your partner off the mat. Try to pull your partner's forehead up towards your own.

Lower your partner to the mat slowly.

Drop back to the kneeling position.

❂ As you stand, post with your arms and shift your weight forward. Doing so will make popping up easier.

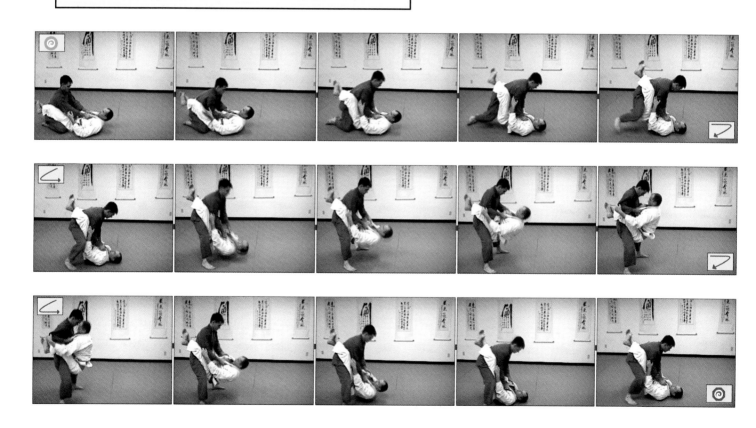

Your partner lays on his back with his knees bent. Bend forward and grab inside your partners knees, thumbs back.

Push your partner's knees to your right and simultaneously cross step your right foot to the outside of your partner's right hip.

Step up with your left foot and post the foot outside your partner's head as you drop your right knee to the knee on belly position.

Step your left leg back to its starting position.

Step your right leg back around to its starting position.

Repeat the drill to the opposite side.

The exercise should be repeated smoothly to the left and right.

◉ Try to do the move smoothly. For that matter, try to do all your drills and techniques smoothly. Constantly iron out the kinks in your movements. There is always some detail you can improve on. Learn to recognize those details.

to be continued...

Tim Cartmell began his martial arts training with the Chinese styles, including ten years of training in China. He has been practicing Brazilian Jiu Jitsu since 1995, and is currently a brown belt under Cleber Luciano. Tim is an Asian Full-Contact tournament champion, and has won several Brazilian Jiu Jitsu tournaments, including the Copa Pacifica at the blue, purple and brown belt levels. Tim is also a submissions grappling tournament winner. Tim Cartmell presently runs the Shen Wu School of Martial Arts in Garden Grove, California.

Ed Beneville is a Brown Belt under sixth degree black belt, Joe Moreira, and has been training Brazilian Jiu-Jitsu since 1996. Ed has entered and won many BJJ tournaments, hi-lights include triple crown (three division) victories – purple belt – at the Grappling Games, Las Vegas, 2001, and at the Grappling Games, Los Angeles, 2001. Ed is an attorney practicing business and contract law in Southern California.